# Idaho Mountain Wildflowers:
## A Photographic Compendium

### Second Edition

# A. Scott Earle
## With Jane Lundin

## Consulting Editor, James L. Reveal

ISBN 10: 1-59152-044-4
ISBN 13: 978-1-59152-044-3

Library of Congress Control Number 2007908608

Larkspur Books
2440 N. Bogus Basin Rd.
Boise, Idaho 83702
Tel. 208 344 0079
larkspur1@cableone.net

Created and designed in the United States.
Produced and distributed by Farcountry Press
P.O. Box 5650, Helena, MT 59604
Tel. 406 444 5100 or 800 821 3874

Printed in China.


Second Edition

Frontispiece:
Marsh marigold, *Caltha leptosepala*, above
the trees (Hyndman Basin, Pioneer Range).

# Contents

## *Introduction to the First Edition*

*Mountain flowers:* The plants illustrated and described in this book are found in three zones: montane, subalpine, and alpine. Montane is the lowest (the word, derived from the French, means, simply, "mountainous"). In central Idaho this lies between about 5,500 to 7500 feet of elevation. Here, stands of fir grow on cooler northern slopes, and lodgepole pine flourishes in the valleys. Higher up, from approximately 7,500 to 10,000 feet, the montane vegetation is replaced by subalpine growth, including spruce, whitebark pine, and subalpine fir. Closer to tree-line, these majestic evergreens gradually undergo a metamorphosis and become stunted, compact, and bush-like, a form known as "krummholz" or "elfin-wood." The alpine zone begins here. The term "alpine flowers" is often used for all mountain flowers. It's better, however, to restrict it to those that grow in the alpine zone—at tree-line and higher. (Yet another zone, where snow persists throughout the year, is found in mountain ranges higher than ours. This, the snow zone, is less rich in flora, but flowering plants do grow there.)

Average temperatures fall about three degrees centigrade for every 1,000 feet of ascent. At higher altitudes, conditions become increasingly harsh, and plants show adaptive changes that protect them against wind and cold. By noting form and growth preferences, one can see how they have adapted to an increasingly inhospitable environment. At 6,000 feet the sticky geranium (*Geranium viscosissimum*), for example, stands erect and its leaves are well separated. The same plant at 9,000 feet is more compact, and "prostrate" (the stem and leaves lie close to the ground). Even though plants tend to be smaller at higher altitudes, their flowers are often as large as those that grow lower down. Many high altitude plants are "pubescent," a term that means "covered with downy hair." As with animals, fur provides insulation. It also helps to retain moisture in the desiccated air higher up. Growing

seasons are short for alpine plants, as snow cover sometimes persists well into July. September brings freezing nights, so growth and reproduction at higher elevations must take place within a two month period. A jump start is required. Extensive and bulky root systems store the nourishment required for rapid growth at the beginning of the next growing season. Similarly, the leaves of many plants at this altitude are evergreen, so photosynthesis can start as soon as snow cover disappears.

Global warming, decreased rainfall, wild fires, land usage, and variations in normal growth cycles influence the number and variety of the wildflowers that one may encounter in our mountains. Effects of change are sometimes not immediately apparent. For example, in 1938 Frank Smythe, one of England's great mountaineers who was also an author, photographer, and a veteran of three pre-World War II Everest expeditions, returned from his ascent of Mana peak (22,481 feet) in the Himalayas. His exit route took him through the flower-filled Bhyundar Valley in northern India, an area previously visited only by native herdsmen. Smythe described this Shangri-La in a classic mountaineering book, *The Valley of Flowers*. Thanks to his book, the Bhyundar Valley became, in time, an Indian national park (Smythe is still revered there). Sheep and goats are no longer permitted to graze in the valley. Lacking their presence, the valley is no longer blanketed with flowers, at least not to the extent that Smythe observed. The mountains of Central Idaho's National Forests were also grazed heavily in the past. Sheep remain, but in reduced numbers. Mountain meadows fertilized with sheep droppings are often covered with of a profusion of fritillaries, paintbrush, elegant camas, and many other wildflowers. With sheep-herding's decline, will our "valleys of flowers" change as did Smythe's?

Increased land use also brings about change. We are seeing algal blooms in our mountain lakes, the result of "enrichment" with animal (horses and dogs, especially) and human waste material. Camping in our National Forests is pretty much unrestricted, and it is not unusual to see tent cities of various organizations—school, scout, church groups, and others—occupying terrain that should be protected. An increasing number of hikers wandering off-trail in sensitive areas also has an impact on plant growth. Weather changes secondary to global warming are having an effect on our native flora. Given these changes, I can only hope that the flowers shown in this book will be around for future generations to enjoy.

***Botanical terms and classification:*** It's just about impossible to avoid using the binomial scientific names of plants, in which the first part designates the genus, and the second part, the species. Common names alone won't do—there's too much duplication and regional variation. As one learns to recognize species of wildflowers, scientific names do become second nature.

I've tried to identify accurately the plants shown here. For some families that is hard to do, and I can only hope that the plant identifications are not too far off. I've used the "Kartesz list," posted on the Internet by the United States Department of Agriculture, for plant names (*http://plants.usda.gov/plants/*). In doing so I've been constantly amazed to see how much at variance that list is with the Hitchcock *et al.* monographic *Vascular Plants of the Pacific Northwest* published in 1969. This is an ongoing phenomenon for, since the '60s, DNA sequencing and chromo-some studies have changed the face of all biology, and taxonomy especially. When plant names have changed, I've indicated the former name parenthetically.

***Using this book:*** Botanists list plant families according to presumed evolutionary emergence. The buttercup family (Ranunculaceae), for example, is relatively primitive and comes before the more evolved sunflower or aster family (Asteraceae) in such a list. Counter to this convention, I have included families alphabetically in the text and in the table of contents. It's a non-botanical way of doing things, but it may make the families easier to find.

I have tried to present representative photographs of various flowers, and, where feasible, include both a close-up of the bloom and a longer view of the entire plant. Many hundreds of species of regional flowering plants are not included in this book. Some bloom infrequently, and we haven't encountered them. Others are so tiny or inconspicuous that they have gone unnoticed. Still others, like the ubiquitous big sagebrush and the dandelion, are so common that there is little point in including them—and occasionally a photograph of an ephemeral bloom just didn't turn out. Given all of the above, this book is by no means a "flora" (a term used for a definitive catalogue of plants). It really isn't a guide book, either, although it can be used as one. I'd prefer to think of it as a photographic compendium of wildflowers encountered during years of hiking and photography in Idaho's mountains.

# Introduction to the Second Edition

Seven years have passed since publication of the first edition of this book. Global warming is now a recognized reality. A half century ago we could not have wandered above tree-line in short-sleeved shirts and short pants, and without parkas in our packs. Since then, valley plants have ascended our mountains: green gentians (*Frasera speciosa*) now grow at tree-line. We cannot remember seeing Lewis's flax (*Linum lewisii*), penstemons (*Penstemon procerus*) and species of Jacob's ladder (*Polemonium viscosum*) growing on alpine tundra, but they are there now.

Recent changes in the classification of plants attest to the march of biologic science. New species names take only a little getting used to; it is harder to adapt to rearrangement of whole families. We have tried to incorporate all of the recent changes, while including previous, more familiar classifications. The reader will also note that authors' names—the names of those who first published descriptions of the various plants—now follow the binomial scientific names at the head of each plant description. We have also added well over two-hundred species, including many true alpine wildflowers. Finally, we have not hesitated to include images and descriptions of non-native wildflowers that may be encountered while hiking in our mountain.

***Acknowledgments***: Two individuals have generously given of their time and knowledge. Their support has been invaluable in bringing this edition into being, and for that I am most grateful.

Jane Lundin—a great trail companion—has made many contributions for which I am most grateful. Blessed with preternaturally sharp eyes, she discovered and accurately identified many of the plants included in this volume. The reader will see her photographs on the following pages. She has read each version of the evolving manuscript, made suggestions, corrected mistakes, and discovered an infinity of typos. This book owes much to her help and encouragement.

Dr. James Reveal, with whom I had the pleasure of working previously on a history of Lewis and Clark's plants, kindly agreed to act as consulting editor for this edition. As noted above, there have been many changes in plant classification—the result of recent molecular, chromosomal and historical studies. As a taxonomist and participant in the ongoing *Flora of North America North of Mexico* project, Jim is uniquely positioned to assist in bringing our plant classifications into agreement with those that have been—or will be—published in the *Flora*. He has read and re-read the manuscript, pointing out errors, offering many suggestions concerning descriptions of various plants, and bringing nomenclature up to date. We have sought to produce a botanically correct work. To the extent that we have succeeded owes much to his generous help and interest.

I wish to thank several botanists who have kindly helped to classify various plants depicted in this book. These include Barbara Ertter (*Potentilla concinnus*), Dave McNeal (*Allium simillimum*), and Guy Nesom (*Symphyotrichum falcatum*). I also appreciate Dr. Karl Holte's kindness in introducing me to the plants of eastern Idaho.

It has been a pleasure to work with Farcountry Press on several projects during the past half dozen years. My thanks to all the folks at Farcountry who were concerned with putting my electronic files on these pages. Thanks especially to Kathy Springmeyer who helped enormously in moving this project forward.

Finally, words can only begin to express my gratitude to Barbara Earle who has shown an extraordinay degree of wifely patience, understanding and support. Without this, there would have been no book.

## Parsley Family (Apiaceae)

The scientific names, Umbelliferae and Apiaceae are both acceptable, although the latter is preferred today by most botanists. There are about 440 genera and 3,590 species in the family. Most are non-woody. Typically their stems are thick and often hollow. Leaves wrap or sheath about the main stem, as in celery or fennel plants, a family characteristic. Small flowers are arranged in flat-topped clusters; the resulting inflorescence resembles the ribs of an inside-out umbrella, the origin of the older family name, Umbelliferae. In some species the flowers heads are compound; i.e., each stemlet divides further. The flowers themselves are almost always radially symmetrical with five small sepals and five petals, although it may take a magnifying glass to make out these details.

Some of the genera contain many similar species, so identification can be difficult, especially as classification is often based on the appearance of the fruit—a technical feature not of much help to amateur botanists. Some species are ornamentals, but the family is valued mostly for its edible plants: carrots, celery, fennel, chervil, parsley, parsnip, etc., as well as herbs used for flavoring including coriander, cumin, caraway, dill, and angelica. Despite the many members that have food value, it is unwise to eat any wild umbellifers unless their identification is certain—several are extremely poisonous. The family name "Apiaceae" was derived from *apium*, the Latin word for parsley.

### Lyall's angelica
### *Angelica arguta* Nutt.

Lyall's angelica is a mountain plant that grows nearly to treeline. It blooms from midsummer on along mountain streams and in nearby wetlands. The name angelica was derived from supposed medicinal properties disclosed by an angel. Our species name, *arguta*, means "sharp-toothed" for the shape of the compound pinnate leaves. The leaf-bearing stems angle outward a bit further at each node, where the leaflets come off, an aid to identifying angelicas. The European plant, *Angelica archangelica* is said to have medicinal value and it is sometimes candied. Use our angelicas and other white-flowered umbellifers at your peril, for they can be hard to distinguish from the poisonous water-hemlock, shown on page 14.

David Lyall (1817-1895), whose name is associated with this plant (formerly it was known as *Angelica lyallii*) was an assistant surgeon and botanist on Captain James Ross's voyage of exploration (1839-1844) to the northern Pacific and arctic regions. Lewis and Clark also collected an angelica (probably this species) along the Lolo Trail in northern Idaho on their outbound journey in 1805 and again on their return journey in 1806. *Angelica arguta* grows only in the Northwest, south to California and Nevada, and in the Canadian provinces of Alberta and British Columbia.

### Waxy spring-parsley
### *Cymopterus glaucus*
### Nutt.

The waxy spring parsley blooms during snow-melt. The low plants hug rocky ground that holds the sun's heat—a favorable microclimate for cold times. The plant grows only in the mountains of Idaho and Montana where it is at home at least as high as treeline. The term *glaucus* is Latin for the waxy bloom seen on some plants, as on the skin of grapes, and on this plant's leaves.

### Snowline spring-parsley
### *Cymopterus nivalis*
### S. Watson

The snowline spring-parsley is a true alpine plant found from treeline to high on the mountain tundra of the alpine zone. It is native to the mountains of Idaho, Montana, Wyoming, and, rarely, to those of Nevada and Oregon. The word *Cymopterus* is derived from two Greek words, *kyma* and *pteron*, meaning "wave-winged," for the plants' winged fruit. These plants' frilly ("bipinnate") leaves are a generic characteristic.

### Western water hemlock
### *Cicuta douglasii* (DC.) J. M. Coult. & Rose

The western water hemlock is, emphatically, not a food plant. The related European hemlock (*Conium maculatum* L., an imported species that now grows throughout the United States) was the plant that poisoned Socrates. Ours would have done just as well, for it is extremely poisonous. It grows in most of the United States and in Canada.

It is a handsome plant with dark green, shiny, three-parted, serrated leaves. Clusters of muddy-white flowers resemble exploding fireworks. The plant grows in Idaho's mountains along streams, and in moist meadows as high as treeline. The stems are hollow and are perfect for making whistles—not a good idea, for the poison reportedly has killed children who did so. It has also been the murder plant of choice in more than one detective novel. The Latin word *Cicuta* originally referred to a now unidentifiable poisonous member of the Parsley family—possibly the European hemlock mentioned above. This species name commemorates David Douglas (1798-1834), he of the fir tree, who is said to have introduced more North American plants into English gardens than any other plant hunter.

### Cow parsnip, *Heracleum maximum* Bartr.

The cow parsnip (formerly *Heracleum lanatum*) is identified by three-parted, coarsely toothed leaves that may grow to be a foot wide, and by an inflorescence made up of numerous umbels that may be as large as the leaves. *Heracleum* refers to Hercules who made use of related plants' supposed medicinal properties. Not only are this plant's leaves unusual for their size (the largest of any American umbellifer), but the flowers also are different from those of other Apiaceae, in that those on the margin of the flowerhead are larger than the others, and their petals are sometimes bilobed. The cow parsnip grows along stream lines, usually in the company of alders, as high as the sub-alpine zone. The plants are said to be edible if the furry stalks are skinned first. Cow parsnips grow throughout North America, excepting the states of the deep south and Texas.

### Nine-leaf biscuit-root
### *Lomatium triternatum* (Pursh) J. M. Coult. & Rose

The nine-leaf lomatium is easily identified by its leaves, as each leaf divides into three narrow leaflets. These, in turn, divide into three more grass-like leaflets (*triternatum*, from the Latin, means "three times three"). Several varieties are recognized, based on minor differences. Ours is var. *triternatum*. It, like the other lomatiums shown here, blooms early in the spring on gravelly slopes and meadows still moist from the snowmelt. This plant occurs in Idaho and every contiguous state as well as in British Columbia, Alberta, and in California. Lewis and Clark collected all three of the lomatiums shown on these pages and several others as well, during the expedition's return journey in the spring of 1806. None had previously been described, hardly surprising for lomatiums are not found east of the Mississippi River.

Frederick Pursh (1775-1820), the botanist who classified the plants returned by Lewis and Clark, described this plant from a specimen gathered along the banks of Idaho's Clearwater River on May 6, 1806. The generic name *Lomatium* is derived from a Greek word that means "fringed," a reference to the appearance of the fruit of some of the species.

### Bare-stemmed biscuit-root
### *Lomatium nudicaule*
### (Pursh) J. M. Coult. & Rose

The bare-stemmed lomatium ("pestle parsnip" is another common name) grows on gravelly slopes as high as treeline. Lewis and Clark collected this plant on April 15, 1806, in the vicinity of The Dalles in today's Oregon. Its species name, *nudicaule*, means, appropriately, "bare-stemmed." Native Americans reputedly used this plant to treat consumption, and "Indian consumption root," has been suggested as a standardized common name. This plant is native to Idaho, the coastal states from California to the province of British Columbia, and in Utah and Nevada.

## Fern-leaf desert-parsley
### *Lomatium dissectum*
### (Nutt.) Mathias & Constance

The fern-leaf desert-parsley (or biscuit root) is a common species of lomatium. There are several varieties. These differ in appearance, but their identical, striped, pumpkin-seed-shaped fruit allows them to be placed in this species. Their divided leaves, (*dissectum* means "divided into many lobes") and their unusually large size—they may be two feet or more tall—will identify the plants as *Lomatium dissectum*; two varieties are shown here. The yellow-flowered plant is *Lomatium dissectum* var. *multifidum* (Nutt.) Mathias & Constance. The varietal name means "much divided." The plant in the inset is *Lomatium dissectum* var. *dissectum*.

Lewis and Clark collected *Lomatium dissectum* on June 10, 1806, near today's Kamiah, Idaho. It can be seen today, lining the walls of the Clearwater Canyon every spring.

### Slender-leaved lovage
### *Ligusticum tenuifolium* S. Watson

Slender leaved lovage, also known as "licorice root," grows only in the Northwest, and neighboring Rocky Mountain states. The plants grow to subalpine elevations in our mountains, although they are not particularly common. Umbels of white flower heads are born atop tall stems. Pinnate (feather-like) compound leaves with narrow, divided leaflets explain the species name, *tenuifolium* ("slender leaf"). As with several other umbellifers, the roots and seeds have a distinctive odor as reflected in the name "licorice-root." The word "lovage" is more properly applied to the edible European plant *Levisticum officinale*. The related European "Scotch lovage" *(Ligusticum scoticum)* was also used in the past for flavoring and as a potherb, reminding one of the close relationship of these plants to other culinary umbellifers such as celery, fennel, and others. This plant and related American species, such as the fern-leaf lovage, *Ligusticum filicinum*, were used by Native Americans in much the same way.

### Great Basin Indian potato
### *Orogenia linearifolia* S. Watson

The Indian potato grows in the foothills and lower mountains of the Great Basin and elsewhere in the Northwest. *Orogenia* is derived from two Greek words; *oros* means "mountain" and *genea* means "race." The species name, *linearifolia*, refers to its narrow leaves. It is a small plant, the umbels are only about a quarter of an inch across. It is remarkable, however, for blooms develop when thousands of plants emerge and flower simultaneously, always in soggy places, as soon as the snow has melted in early spring. Common names, "Indian potato" and "turkey peas" refer to its edible roots. The round to radish-shaped roots are pea-sized or a bit larger. They are tasty (unusual, for many "edible" plants are not) and may be eaten cooked or raw. Plant-hunter Sereno Watson (1826-1892) discovered the two umbellifers shown on this page while a member of the King Expedition.

**Apiaceae**

### Western sweet cicely
### *Osmorhiza occidentalis* (Nutt. ex Torr. & A. Gray) Torr.

Crush this plant's flowers and smell their fragrance—indubitably licorice! Although true licorice is derived from another plant, *Glycorrhiza glabra*, a member of the pea family, the odor is the same. Our plant is easily identified not only by its distinctive fragrance, but also by deep green three-parted lanceolate leaves and rather dainty yellow flowers; the latter borne in a lacy umbel. Despite the name "sweet cicely," osmorhizas are not true cicelys (or chervils), although they are in the same family, and may also be used for flavoring. The western sweet cicely is common throughout our mountain West, and in the western Canadian provinces of Alberta and British Columbia.

### Mountain sweet cicely
### *Osmorhiza berteroi* DC.

Three-part, compound, deep-green, toothed leaves and tiny white flowers borne in an umbel characterize this ubiquitous plant. It is found in almost every state and Canadian province growing from sea-level, to mid-elevations. The roots and flowers of most osmorhizas have a pronounced licorice-like odor (the generic name, *Osmorhiza*, derived from the Greek, means "fragrant-root"). This species, however, is odorless, so on first encounter one would hardly suspect that it belonged to the genus *Osmorhiza*. The species name, *berteroi*, honors an Italian physician, Carlo Giuseppe Bertero (1789-1831).

### Northern yampah
### *Perideridia montana* (Blank.) Dorn

The northern, or common yampah (false caraway is an alternate name), grows in all of the Rocky Mountain states as well as in Nevada, the four states of the Northwest, south to California and east to the Black Hills of South Dakota. As with species of *Angelica* and *Ligusticum*, it blooms in mid-summer or later on the banks of mountain streams. It is also most likely the edible plant—"a speceis of fennel"—that Meriwether Lewis (1774-1809) saw being harvested on August 26th near the Lemhi Pass on today's Idaho-Montana border (where, interestingly, yampah is no longer found). Evidently he did not collect a specimen, or if he did, it did not survive the journey, for yampah is not represented in the Lewis and Clark Herbarium in Philadelphia.

### Swamp white-heads
### *Sphenosciadium capitellatum* A. Gray

Swamp white-heads are tall plants—three or four feet high—found along streams and in moist meadows, from foothills to mountain valleys, blooming in mid- to late summer. They are easily identified by their woolly flowerheads, each made up of many tiny flowers. The attractive little heads are usually white, but sometimes have a pinkish tinge. The leaves are compound, made up of three or more parts. It is the only species in the genus *Sphenosciadium*, found only in Idaho, Nevada, Oregon, and California. So far as we are aware, swamp white-heads have no use as a food plant. The scientific name is derived from the Greek words *sphena* meaning "wedge," and *skiada* for "parasol," referring respectively to its wedge shaped fruits and the plant's umbels. The species' name, *capitellatum,* means "little heads." Alternate common names include "rangers' buttons," and "woolly-headed parsnip."

## Dogbane Family (Apocynaceae)

Recent taxonomic revisions have joined the dogbane family (Apocynaceae) with the milkweed family (Asclepiadaceae) while retaining the former name for the combined family. The change in classification did not come as a surprise to botanists, for there are obvious similarities between dogbanes and milkweeds. Both exude thick milky latex when injured, both have fiber-containing seedpods, and plants in both families contain poisons. There are, in addition, technical similarities of importance to botanists. As a result of this taxonomic shuffling, the reconstituted dogbane family is considerably larger, made up of approximately 480 genera and 4,800 species. Most grow in the tropics; many are vines, some are trees.

The combined family has considerable economic importance. Not uncommonly plant poisons have therapeutic value, and this is true of the Apocynaceae. The anti-hypertensive drug reserpine, for example, is derived from the *Rauwolfia* tree; the anti-cancer drugs vincristine and vinblastine come from periwinkle plants (*Vinca* spp.); strophanthin, a cardiac stimulant, is extracted from species of *Strophanthus*. Others are important ornamentals including species of milkweed (*Asclepias* spp.), oleander (*Nerium* spp.), periwinkle, and the frangipangi tree (*Plumeria*) to list a few. The family is also economically important, producing timber from trees, fiber for cordage, and latex derivatives for various uses.

Both "milkweed" and "dogbane" are old terms. The OED's citations are from 1598 for milkweed and a year earlier, 1597, for dogbane, citing Gerard's *Herbal* for the latter; "Dogs bane is a deadly and dangerous plant, especially to fower footed beasts." Species of both plants grow in our mountains. Several are shown here.

### Spreading dogbane
### *Apocynum androsaemifolium* **L.**

The spreading dogbane is a loose vine-like plant that spreads along the ground, usually blooming in mid-summer. It is often found in the open shade of evergreen forests from mid-elevations to subalpine slopes. Spreading dogbane is easy to identify by its growth habit, by its bright green, smooth surfaced, opposite leaves, and by attractive little pink flowers bearing more or less reflexed (bent back) petals. Pick a leaf and you will see the distinctive thick white sap (latex) common to plants in this family. Spreading dogbane grows throughout North America, excepting in several southern states. In common with most plants that Linnaeus described (the meaning of "L." following the binomial scientific name above), spreading dogbane also occurs in Europe; most likely it is the plant Gerard termed "dogs bane" (see the preceding page).

Hemp dogbane, or Indian hemp, *Apocynum cannabinum* (not shown) is a related, similar species that also grows in Idaho (and in every state and in most Canadian provinces) preferring disturbed or previously cultivated ground at lower elevations. Native Americans used the fuzzy fiber contained in the plant's seedpod to make cordage, explaining its common names.

### Showy milkweed (left, left below)
#### *Asclepias speciosa* Torr.

The showy milkweed's range extends eastward from the Pacific coastal states to midwestern United States and Canada. The plant grows on moist soil and along slowly moving waterways. Its general appearance, attractive flower clusters, milky sap, and, later, the typical milkweed pods, all make the plant easy to identify. The genus *Asclepias* is named for the Greek physician and minor deity, Asculapius. The plant's species name, *speciosa*, is from the Latin and means "showy" or "handsome."

### Narrow-leaf milkweed (above)
#### *Asclepias fascicularis* Dcne.

The narrow-leaf milkweed is a western plant, found in Idaho—where it seems to be uncommon—in Utah, and westward to the Pacific coastal states. The plant may be identified by its narrow, opposite leaves and by two or more crowded umbels of dark, reddish-purple flowers borne on short stems that arise from the axils of upper leaves.* The fruit (not shown) is a long pod. The species name *fascicularis*, from the Latin, means "clustered" referring to the flowers.

---

\* The term "axil" as used in this context refers to the upper angle where a leaf arises from the main stem. *Cf.* "axilla," the anatomical word for the armpit.

# Aster, or Composite Family (Asteraceae)

The common names for this family: sunflower, composite, and aster family; and the scientific names Compositae, and Asteraceae, are all correct, although the terms "aster family" and "Asteraceae" are preferred today. It is the largest family of flowering plants, made up of 1,530 genera and 23,800 species. All family members have a common characteristic: each bloom or flowerhead (commonly referred to as the plant's flower) is made up of many tiny flowers. Those in the center of the flowerhead are "disk flowers," and those on the edge, each with a single strap-like petal, are "ray flowers." In some species ray flowers occupy the entire flowerhead; conversely, others have only disk flowers. The Asteraceae have other characteristics that can help with identification. These include protruding Y-shaped styles; multiple pointed small leaves, or "bracts" (collectively forming an "involucre") that cup each flowerhead; and often a feathery "pappus" attached to each seed that aids in seed dissemination (as, notably, with dandelions). It is not always easy to recognize members of the aster family for some flowerheads may be tiny, resemble those of other plants, or are in other ways atypical.

Many of the Asteraceae are cultivated as garden ornamentals: zinnias, chrysanthemums, daisies, and asters, to name a few. Some are important food plants: lettuce and other greens, artichoke, and the food-oils obtained from sunflowers and safflowers. Still others are troublesome weeds: ragweed, knapweed, thistles, burdock, common dandelion, and many others. It would take a book to describe all of the Asteraceae that grow in Idaho; the ones pictured here can only serve as a representative sampling of the many that grow in our mountains.

**Asters, *Aster* L.**

Until recently many of our plants were classified as species of *Aster,* a genus that is now represented by several smaller genera. It may help to think of the species formerly in genus *Aster* as "aster-related plants" (or maybe "asteroids?") an informal classification supported by many common names that have "aster" in them. This group of plants have the following common characteristics that separate them from the fleabanes (*Erigeron* spp.): they bloom later, they tend to be purple-rayed, and they have "shingled" bracts lined up in irregular rows under their flower heads.

### Leafy aster
### *Symphyotrichum foliaceum* (Lindl. ex DC.) G. L. Nesom
### var. *apricum* (A. Gray) G. L. Nesom

The leafy aster, a tall plant, is found throughout the West, blooming from mid-summer on. The plants have large, stemmed, basal leaves and smaller "clasping" (stemless) leaves higher up. Each stem bears one flowerhead, most commonly with fifteen rays. As the flowers mature, the central bright yellow disk becomes brownish, and the petals darken to a rich, deep purple—a distinguishing feature. Several varieties are recognized by minor differences in their morphology. Var. *apricum,* ("*apricum*" means "sun-loving") shown here, has purple-margined bracts (the small leaflets that cup the flowerhead). It is a common plant along our trails.

### Alpine aster
### *Oreostemma alpigenum*
### (Torr. & A. Gray) Greene
### var. *haydenii* (Porter) G. L. Nesom

The alpine aster is a subalpine to alpine species that grows in clusters in open spaces. It is found in the northwestern states and in Nevada and California. Botanists recognize three varieties; only this one grows in Idaho. The plant has a basal crown of linear gray-green leaves. These, the stem, and purple-tinged bracts are covered with fine hair. The generic name *Oreostemma,* derived from two Greek words, means "mountain crown." To avoid confusion with other alpine asters the name "tundra mountain crown" has been suggested for this plant.

## Rocky Mountain aster
### *Ionactis stenomeres*
### (A. Gray) Greene

The Rocky Mountain aster's attractive flowerheads bear thirteen (occasionally more) narrow rays. The word *stenomeres,* from the Greek, means "narrow-parts" presumably referring to the rays and to narrow, same-sized leaves that ascend the stem. *Ionactis* is also derived from the Greek, and means "violet rays" (*cf.* "actinic"). The Rocky Mountain aster grows only in Idaho, Montana, Washington and the province of Alberta.

## White prairie aster
### *Symphyotrichum falcatum*
### (Lindl.) G. L. Nesom

The white prairie aster is distinguished by clusters of white flowerheads that tend to be borne on the same side of tall stems. The plants spread by short rhizomes which also contributes to their clustered appearance. Although commonly found on the plains, the plants also grow in our mountains. This one was photographed just west of Lolo Pass in north central Idaho. The name, *falcatum,* means "sickle-shaped." It is not clear why it was applied to this plant.

**Elegant aster**
*Eucephalus perelegans*
**(A. Nelson &J. F. Macbr.) W. A. Weber**

The elegant aster blooms from mid-summer on, growing as high as the subalpine zone. Its five (occasionally eight) rays, make it quite distinctive. The elegant aster was collected in 1834 and described in 1841 by botanist Thomas Nuttall (1786-1839) who had recently resigned from the faculty of Harvard College to join Boston businessman, Nathaniel Wyeth (1802-1856, for whom the *Wyethia* was named) on a journey west to Oregon. The plant grows from Oregon to Montana and south to Nevada, Utah and Colorado.

**Hoary aster**
*Machaeranthera canescens* var. *canescens*
**(Pursh) A. Gray**

The name *Machaeranthera* was derived from two Greek words meaning "sword" and "anther," for the plant's sharp-pointed anthers. The hoary aster blooms in summer's heat, from the end of July through August into September, in dry places. A furry stem (the Latin *canescens* implies "covered with gray hairs"), spiny bracts, variably white-based to fully purple rays and an orange disk help to identify the plant. Meriwether Lewis collected a hoary aster (var. *incana*) on the Columbia River in October, 1805, near today's The Dalles, Oregon.

**Alpine aster**
***Ionactis alpina***
**(Nutt.) Greene**

One of the problems with common names is that they are often duplicated; there are, for example, several "alpine asters." The one shown here grows in large clumps on dry ground, usually in the company of sagebrush, as high as the subalpine zone. Characterized by small, clustered gray-green leaves and thirteen or so rays, it is found in Idaho, Montana, Utah, Oregon and Nevada. It was previously classified as *Aster scopulorum*.

**Fleabanes or daisies, *Erigeron* species**, differ from the "asteroids" in several ways; most notably, they bloom earlier, and the bracts that subtend the flower are regular in configuration The name, *Erigeron*, derived from the Greek (*eri+geron*) means "early-old-man"—fleabanes bloom early and have grayish, hairy foliage. The botanically preferred common name "fleabane" was derived centuries ago because several daisy-like plants, notably species of *Chrysanthemum* and *Tanacetum*, contain insecticidal pyrethrins.

**Bear River fleabane**
***Erigeron ursinus* D. C. Eaton**

The Bear River fleabane is larger and showier than most erigerons. It is characterized by a basal cluster of narrow lanceolate leaves, and narrow stem leaves. The stem is stout, bearing a single flowerhead. A broad yellow disk is surrounded by 100 or so purple rayflowers. The plant is found in eastern Idaho, western Montana, Utah, Colorado and Wyoming. The Bear River, from which the plant's common name was derived, flows from Utah's Wasatch Range to Bear Lake on the Idaho-Montana border, and thence to the Great Salt Lake. The Latin species name, *ursinus*, means "bear."

### Idaho Fleabane
### *Erigeron asperugineus*
### (D. C. Eaton) A. Gray

The Idaho fleabane is a lovely little subalpine plant that blooms in early summer. The name *asperugineus* means "rough" referring to the plant's brittle-feeling stems and crisped leaves. It occurs in northern Nevada (where it was first collected), but is more common in Idaho, especially in the mountains of the central part, and in western Montana.

### Showy daisy
### *Erigeron speciosus*
### (Lindl.) DC.

The showy daisy is a common plant in our mountains where it grows in large clusters crowded with many flowerheads. These are about two inches across, with 60 to 150 narrow rays that range in color from purple to nearly white. Alternate lanceolate leaves ascend the stem. Showy daisies are distributed throughout the Rocky Mountains and the Northwest. "Aspen daisy" has been suggested as a standardized common name for the plant. David Douglas introduced the showy daisy into England and it is grown there today as an ornamental. The name *speciosus* means "splendid."

### Dwarf mountain (or cutleaf) daisy
### *Erigeron compositus* Pursh

The dwarf mountain (or cutleaf) daisy is a miniature plant that grows on rocky ground and exposed slopes. While it grows at all elevations, it thrives as an alpine plant, growing at treeline and higher. Typically it forms compact clumps that bloom from mid-spring to mid-summer according to the elevation. The plant grows in most western states, through Canada to Alaska, and east to Greenland. Lewis and Clark were the first to collect the cutleaf daisy, possibly in the fall of 1805 (as a dry plant), or in the spring of 1806 while they were camped on the Clearwater River near today's Kamiah, Idaho. Because it is both attractive and hardy this little plant is used as an "alpine" in rock gardens. The name, *compositus* means "compound" referring to its three-parted, or "ternate," leaves, made up of deeply divided leaflets.

### Evermann's fleabane
### *Erigeron evermannii* Rydb.

Evermann's daisy is a good-sized composite with basal lanceolate leaves a bare, furry stem and a single flowerhead. It is a true mountain plant, one that is found only at high elevations in Idaho, Montana (where it is rare), and Alberta. Its rays are sometimes tinged blue or pink, although ours are usually white, as shown here. Barton Warren Evermann (1853-1932) was a naturalist, best known as an ichthyologist. He published an important ichthyological text, *Fishes of North and Middle America* in 1900.

Jane Lundin

## Coulter's daisy
### *Erigeron coulteri* Porter

Coulter's daisy resembles Evermann's daisy in that a single white-rayed flowerhead is borne on each stem. It differs, however, because its stems are not bare but have several to many lanceolate leaves that become clasping (stemless) as they ascend the stem. There are also more rayflowers—usually from 40 to 100, whereas Evermann's daisy usually has 40 or fewer. Coulter's daisy grows at higher altitudes, often along streams, and is present in all of the Rocky Mountain States, and in Nevada and California.

John Merle Coulter, (1851-1928), for whom the plant is named started his career as botanist to a geological expedition that explored the Rocky Mountains in 1872-73. He later became an academic, holding chairs in botany at several colleges. He is known today for his comprehensive *Manual of Rocky Mountain Botany* (1885).

## Mountain townsendia
### *Townsendia alpigena* Piper

The townsendias are closely related to the fleabanes. The mountain townsendia shown here is a small alpine rock plant that grows at or above treeline in the mountains of Idaho, Montana, Wyoming, Utah, Oregon and rarely in Nevada. The plants are characterized by relatively large flowerheads borne singly on longish stems. Their central disks are prominent, and the rays range from a light purple color (usually) to near white. Its small, ovoid, basal leaves are covered with fine hair and the involucral bracts below the flowerhead are striped, a distinguishing feature. Twenty seven species of *Townsendia* are now recognized; none grow east of the Mississippi River.

David Townsend (1787-1858), for whom the genus was named, was an amateur Pennsylvania botanist.

Jane Lundin

### Heartleaf arnica
### *Arnica cordifolia* Hook.

While the origin of the generic name *Arnica* is unknown, this plant's species name, *cordifolia,* makes sense, for it means "heart-shaped leaf" and its leaves are unmistakably that shape. It is one of our commonest mountain composites. The plants bloom from late spring until mid-summer according to altitude. They prefer the open shade of evergreen forests, but occasionally overflow onto neighboring meadows. Typically, the stems lie close to the ground (they are "prostrate"), turning upward to flower. Eight to thirteen wide, pointed, bright yellow-orange rays are borne on each flowerhead. Heartleaf arnicas grows in much of the West, ranging from the Yukon Territory to New Mexico.

### Streambank arnica
### *Arnica lanceolata* Nutt.
### var. *prima* (Maguire) Strother & S. J. Wolf

Arnicas are not difficult to identify, at least at the generic level. Their flowerheads are borne at the end of one to several stems and are fairly large with eight to fifteen bright yellow rays and a well defined, rounded ("turbinate") disk. Opposing leaves—an identifying feature—are given off at intervals along the stem; in some species the leaves also form a basal cluster. The streambank arnica resembles several similar species. It is tall, thin-stemmed and, as its common name suggests, grows along mountain streams, typically at high elevations. It is easily identified, both by where it grows and by the stemless leaves that "clasp" the main stem (*amplexicaulis*, means "stem-embracing").

The sap of arnicas may irritate; tincture of arnica, usually derived from the European plant, *Arnica montana*, has been used for centuries as a rubifacient, an external application useful for treating painful sprains and bruises.

This plant was formerly classified as *Arnica amplexicaulis* Nutt., and is so classified in older guide books.

### Twin arnica
### *Arnica sororia* Greene

The twin arnica takes its species name from the Latin word for "sister" presumably because two (or more) flowerheads arise from a common stem. It is a meadow plant, growing to fairly high elevations; it may be identified by this growth habit, by its cluster of large basal leaves and smaller opposed, lanceolate, stem leaves. The twin arnica is closely related to a similar, taller and larger-leaved species (shining arnica, *Arnica fulgens* Pursh; not shown) that has much the same range throughout our western mountain states and Canadian provinces. The two are so closely related that until recently the species shown here was considered to be a varietal form of the larger plant.

### Slender arnica
### *Arnica gracilis* Rydb.

*Arnica gracilis* (formerly *Arnica latifolia* var. *gracilis*) is a plant whose habit—cluster-forming, low-growing, nestled among rocks—is typical of many other alpine and subalpine plants. As illustrated, it is at home on rocky ground. The rocks protect the plants and hold the sun's heat. By looking at the plants closely, one can see that small, broadly lanceolate leaves arise opposite each other, typical of arnicas in general. The slender arnica is found in the mountains of all of the northwestern states and provinces, and south to Wyoming, Colorado, and Utah.

### Spear-leaf arnica
### *Arnica longifolia* D. C. Eaton

The spear-leaf arnica is a high altitude, cluster-forming composite. It blooms in mid-August, usually close to water: near seep springs, lakes, and slow-moving streams. The plant's preference for sheltering rocks, its proximity to water, and its long, opposing, pointed leaves (responsible for both common and specific names) set it apart from other high altitude clustered composites. The shrubby goldenweed (page 39) is the plant it most closely resembles. The leaves of both plants are sticky and both give off an odor when crushed. The medicinal odor of the arnica's leaves is not nearly as strong, however, as that of the highly aromatic goldenweed.

The spearleaf arnica is native to all of the central and northern Rocky Mountain states, as well as in Nevada, California, Alberta and British Columbia, although it is rare in the Canadian provinces.

### Mountain (or false) dandelion, *Agoseris glauca* (Pursh) Raf.

Even though it lacks a central disk and is somewhat similar in appearance to a dandelion (*Taraxacum officinale*), the mountain dandelion is not closely related to the weed. The mountain dandelion is characterized by a long bare stem, a terminal flowerhead, and a few linear leaves that spring from a basal rosette. Two varieties are recognized based on relatively minor differences (width and shape of leaves, plant size, etc.). Ours is var. *glauca*. The plant grows at all elevations, as high as treeline. The terms "mountain dandelion," or simply "agoseris" are used for the plant. Because *agoseris* was derived from two Greek words that mean "goat-chicory," a common name of "pale goat-chicory" has been suggested for the plant. The species is widely distributed throughout the western states, east to the Great Lakes and north to Yukon.

### Orange mountain dandelion *Agoseris aurantiaca* (Hook.) Greene

The orange agoseris is a relatively uncommon plant that you'll see from time to time during the summer months, usually at higher elevations. It is an eye-catcher because of its burnt orange hue, unusual among Asteraceae in our area.

The species name *aurantiaca*, from the Latin, means "orange-red" (the word is cognate with "orange"). Its leaves are a bit wider than the agoseris shown above, but otherwise the two are similar. This plant also grows in the western mountain states, north to Alaska and western Canadian provinces, west to the Pacific coast, and south to California and New Mexico. The ungainly term "orange-flower goat-chicory" has been suggested as a standardized name.

**Arrowleaf balsamroot**
***Balsamorhiza sagittata***
**(Pursh) Nutt.**

This robust and ubiquitous plant grows in most western states and provinces, from sea level to treeline. Its clustered, arrow-shaped, gray-green leaves and showy flowerheads make it easy to identify. The plants bloom from spring into mid-summer on ever higher mountainsides. The common and scientific names were derived from its arrow-shaped leaves and balsam-like odor of its roots. Native Americans used its roots and shoots for food. Lewis and Clark twice gathered specimens of balsamroot in the spring and summer of 1806.

**Largeleaf balsamroot**
***Balsamorhiza macrophylla*** **Nutt.**

Although the arrowleaf is by far the most prevalent species of balsamroot, there are nine other western species. The largeleaf balsamroot (also cutleaf balsamroot) is a Great Basin species, crossing into Idaho. It is similar to the arrowleaf balsamroot, differing chiefly in the shape of its large, incised, pinnate leaves. The species name, from the Greek, reflects its common name, "large-leaf."

**Hooker's balsamroot**
***Balsamorhiza hookeri*** **(Hook.) Nutt.**
**var.** ***hispidula*** **(Sharp) Cronquist**

Hooker's balsamroot is found in many places in the West. Six varieties are recognized; some are quite localized in distribution. The variety shown here grows in south-central Idaho and south into Utah and Nevada. It is a small plant with pinnate (feather-like) leaves. Its stems and leaves are hairy, as its name *hispidula* (covered with stiff hairs) suggests.

### Scabland fleabane
### *Erigeron bloomeri* A. Gray

The scabland fleabane is usually found growing in barren, rocky sites in the mountains and foothills of Idaho, Nevada, Utah and the Pacific coastal states. As the illustration suggests, it is characterized by narrow basal leaves and naked stems that each bear a single rayless flowerhead. The species name honors an eminent California botanist, Dr. Hiram Green Bloomer (1819-1874), who collected the plant in Nevada, near Virginia City.

### Line-leaf daisy
### *Erigeron linearis*
### (Hook.) Piper

The line-leaf daisy (also known as the desert yellow fleabane) is, like the cutleaf daisy shown on page 29, a small plant that grows in discrete clumps. It prefers exposed gravelly slopes where it often grows in profuse numbers from late spring into the summer, as high as treeline. As with many plants that are adapted to dry places, both leaves and stems feel brittle. The common and scientific species names describe its thin "linear" leaves. The line-leaf daisy is restricted to the northern Rocky Mountains (including British Columbia) and western coastal states.

**Common sunflower**
*Helianthus annuus* L.

The common sunflower, originally native to North America, has now spread throughout the world. The plant is immediately recognized by its large flowerhead, broad hairy leaves and tall stems. *Helianthus*, is from the Greek words for "sun" and "flower"; *annuus*, is Latin for "annual" (botanical names often mix Greek and Latin). Sunflowers bloom from mid-summer on, and are common in Idaho, growing at least as high as the montane zone in open fields, along fencelines and roadsides. Sunflowers have long been cultivated for their seeds, and more recently for the oil that the seeds contain. Various sunflowers are considered weeds in some parts of the United States.

**Nuttall's sunflower**
*Helianthus nuttallii* Torr. & A. Gray

The genus Helianthus is a large one, made up of sixty-seven species and many varieties; several grow in Idaho. Nuttall's sunflower is a fairly common, tall, perennial plant characterized by sunflower-like flowerheads and narrow, lanceolate, mostly opposed leaves. The plants prefer moist or recently moist soil, and grow to fairly high elevations in our mountains. They are found in all our western states, excepting several in the south, and in all of the lower Canadian provinces, east to Quebec. Two other varieties are recognized and are known by their varietal names in other parts of the country.

**Rocky Mountain dwarf sunflower**
*Helianthella uniflora* (Nutt.) Torr. & A. Gray

When Thomas Nuttall published the first description of this plant in 1834, he classified it as a species of sunflower, *Helianthus uniflora*. Later, it was reclassified as its own genus, *Helianthella* (the diminutive of *Helianthus*). Typically the dwarf sunflower has several long stems that arise from a thickened, persistent base ("caudex"). Large, opposing, lanceolate leaves are given off at intervals along the stems, each topped by a single (*uniflora*) sunflower-like flowerhead. Although this plant is not a high altitude species, although it may be found in the foothills and lower mountain ranges in Idaho and other Rocky Mountain and Pacific coastal states, north to British Columbia south to California, Arizona and New Mexico.

### Curly cup gumweed
### *Grindelia squarrosa* (Pursh) Dunal
### var. *quasiperennis* Lunell

The curly cup gumweed is an odd plant, because its flower cups contain a viscous, resinous fluid. Native Americans used the resin to treat skin conditions, and respiratory problems. The leaves were used for tea, and the buds were chewed as gum. The Latin species name, *squarrosa*, means "bent at right angles," referring to bracts that turn outward at the base of the heads forming a "curlycup." Gumweeds grow along mountain roadsides, often in great numbers, blooming from early to mid-summer. The name *Grindelia* honors David Hieronymus Grindel (1776-1836) a Russian botanist. Gumweeds grow throughout the United States, except in a few southern states; the plants are also found in Canada and in Mexico. Lewis and Clark collected another variety of this plant in present day Nebraska on August 17, 1804.

### Indian blanket-flower
### *Gaillardia aristata* Pursh

The Indian blanket-flower, or gaillardia, is native to Idaho and the other Rocky Mountain states, west to California and east across the country in the nothern tier states and in the Canadian provinces. Meriwether Lewis collected this species in today's Montana, near the Continental Divide on July 7, 1806. The plant is easily identified by its reddish brown-based, three-lobed rays and its bristly, reddish-brown disk (*aristata* means "bristly"). The name *Gaillardia* honors an 18th century French magistrate, Gaillard de Merentonneau (also spelled Charentonneau), who had an interest in botany. *Gaillardia aristata* is often confused with the colorful firewheel, *Gaillardia pulchella*, a common garden plant that may escape and persist locally in our area for several seasons.

**Shrubby goldenweed**
*Ericameria suffruticosa* (Nutt.) **G. L. Nesom**

The shrubby goldenweed (formerly *Haplopappus suffruticosus*) is a summer-blooming plant that grows as high as treeline, sometimes turning barren, south-facing slopes bright yellow. The flowerheads are few-rayed (5-9) with bristly central disks. Crisp-edged leaves are covered with fine hair. The plants have a very strong, but not unpleasant aromatic odor that may fill the air even before the plants have bloomed. The shrubby goldenweed grows in the northern Rocky Mountains south to Colorado and west to California.

**Green rabbitbrush**
*Chrysothamnus viscidiflorus* (Hook.) **Nutt.**

The green rabbitbrush is not as striking as the rubber rabbitbrush (on the following page) although it is also part of the mid- to late summer landscape in much of the West. There are five different varieties of *Chrysothamnus viscidiflorus*; three grow in Idaho. The differences between varieties are relatively minor. All are crowded, clustered plants with woody stems and variably hairy, narrow green leaves. The stems, leaves and flowers often feel sticky, explaining the name *viscidiflorus*. Narrow, discoid, brush-like flowers characterize rabbitbrushes in general. Rayless composites are uncommon in the East; this may have prompted Meriwether Lewis to collect six specimens of rabbitbrushes. The plants' aromatic medicinal odor may also have suggested, erroneously, that rabbitbrushes have medicinal value.

### Rubber Rabbitbrush
#### *Ericameria nauseosa* (Pallas ex Pursh) G. L. Nesom & G. I. Baird

There are twenty-two varieties of *Ericameria nauseosa* (formerly *Chrysothamnus nauseosus*). Add several other species also known as rabbitbrushes, and one ends up with a taxonomic jumble. We'll consider the plant shown here as representative and leave it at that. The rubber rabbitbrush has clusters of rayless, bright yellow flowerheads, and frosted blue-green linear leaves. The sticky latex-like sap is white, explaining the name, "rubber rabbitbrush." Meriwether Lewis was also confused by the rabbitbrushes, the likes of which he had never before encountered—not surprising for it was then unknown to science—and he collected two specimens of this plant. A late bloomer, the rabbitbrush adds bright late summer color to drab sage-covered hillsides. The plant is found throughout the Great Plains and western states, north to adjacent Canadian provinces, and south to Mexico.

### Low hawksbeard
### *Crepis modocensis* Greene

The low hawksbeard has only ray flowers. Its leaves are deeply incised, long-stemmed, and pinnate (feather-like). The Greek word *krepis* means "sandal," apparently used by Theophrastus for a similar plant. The name, *modocensis*, refers to Modoc County in California. Other *Crepis* species also grow in Idaho; the form of their deeply serrated leaves helps to identify them, although a tendency to cross-breed may make identification difficult. *Crepis modocensis* is native to the three western coastal states and east through the Rocky Mountains.

The etymology of the name "hawksbeard" is obscure. Possibly because the seed pappus is bristly it suggested the "mustache" feathers of night-hawks (nightjar family, Caprimulgidae).

### Western hawkweed
### *Hieracium scouleri* Hook.

Hawkweed's generic name was derived from the Greek *hierax* for "hawk." The half inch wide flowerheads are without disk florets. All parts of the plant save the flowerhead itself are notably hairy and the sap is milky—helpful in identification. The western hawkweed is a common plant that blooms from mid-summer on as high as the subalpine zone. Interestingly, Gregor Johan Mendel (1822-1884) attempted to repeat his genetic experiments—originally carried out with pea plants—using a species of *Hieracium*. He did not know that hawkweeds may reproduce asexually by a process known as "apomyxis." His results were so inconsistent that he gave up on further plant experimentation. John Scouler (1804-1871) was a naturalist who visited the Northwest briefly in 1825-6.

### Common eriophyllum
### *Eriophyllum lanatum* (Pursh) J. Forbes

Various common names including "woolly sunflower" have been suggested for this attractive composite, but it is usually known simply as an "eriophyllum" (*eri-OFF-illum*). It is distributed widely in the West, and a dozen or so varieties are recognized (ours is var. *integrifolium* (Hook.) Smiley, characterized by "entire" [unlobed] leaves and seven or eight wide rays). The leaves are covered with fine hairs giving them a silvery color, explaining the species name, *lanatum* ("woolly"). Eriophyllums prefer meadows and other open areas. They grow to subalpine elevations, blooming from late spring on. Lewis and Clark saw eriophyllums above their camp on the Clearwater River near present day Kamiah, Idaho, where they gathered two specimens on June 6, 1806; the plant was then unknown to science.

**Black-hairy prairie dandelion**
*Nothocalaïs nigrescens*
**(L. H. Hend.) A. Heller**

As their common names suggest, the prairie dandelion, the mountain dandelions, and several other yellow-rayed plants have inflorescenses that resemble those of the common dandelion. They all have common characerics: milky juice, taproots, dandelion-like pappuses, and they lack diskflowers.* Despite this plant's common name, "prairie-dandelion," it is a mountain plant that grows only near the common borders of Wyoming, Montana and Idaho. The Latin species name, *nigrescens,* means "turning black," for dark markings on the involucral bracts, the pointed leaves that cup the flower parts.

---

* Some of these dandelion-like species have been reclassified several times. The plant shown here was originally published as *Microseris nigrescens*, joining a few other plants in the genus *Microseris*. Some of these have recently been reclassified as *Nothocalaïs*, a name coined by Asa Gray (1810-1888) of Harvard College, a man who made his reputation naming plants that others collected. Needless to say, reclassifications can be confusing, not only to lay plant-lovers, but to many botanists as well.

Calaïs was a minor Greek god, son of Borealis, the north wind. The prefix *notho-* means "false" suggesting that the genus was similar to, but not the same as *Calaïs* (today's genus *Uropappus*).

### Rocky Mountain Canada goldenrod
### *Solidago lepida* DC. var. *salebrosa* (Piper) Semple

The goldenrod shown here is found from British Columbia, east to Saskatchewan, and south to Arizona and New Mexico. It grows in open places to fairly high elevations from mid-summer on, usually in open meadows. Its varietal name, *salebrosa*, means "rough," for the surface of the plant's leaves. If you examine the plant's bloom closely, you'll find that it is made up of hundreds of tiny composite flowerheads, and that each of these little heads has ray flowers less than a tenth of an inch in size. The generic name *Solidago* was derived from two Latin words, *solidus* meaning "complete" and *ago* for "I make whole," because the European goldenrod (*Solidago virgaurea*) was, in times gone by, valued as a "vulnerary"—a substance able to heal external wounds.

### Mountain goldenrod
### *Solidago multiradiata* Aiton

The rays are more obvious on the mountain goldenrod than those on the plant shown above. It is a summer-blooming plant, often seen along our trails where the ground is moist. As its common name suggests, it is only encountered at higher elevations; in Idaho it grows at least as high as treeline. In common with many of our alpine plants this one occurs at progressively lower elevations as one goes further north in its range—Canada, Alaska and Siberia. There are several varieties of mountain goldenrod, although this is the only one found in Idaho. While the common name "mountain goldenrod" describes the plant as it grows in the West, it is not wholly accurate for the same plant also grows in Labrador and southeastern Canada at sea level.

### Alpine hulsea
### *Hulsea algida* A. Gray

The alpine hulsea is an attractive yellow composite that—like the hymenoxys shown below—has adapted to living at tree-line. It grows in well protected crevices on talus slopes where it flowers in mid- to late summer. Serrated leaves, a thick stem and a yellow flowerhead suggest a common dandelion, but a closer look shows that its leaves are thick and the flowerhead has both ray and disk-flowers. Its sticky leaves, like those of many composites, give off a pronounced aromatic odor when crushed. This is the only hulsea found in Idaho. (A dwarf species, *Hulsea nana,* is native to the Cascade and Sierra Nevada ranges.)

Hulseas were named for United States Army physician and botanist, Dr. Gilbert White Hulse (1807-1883). The Latin word *algida* means "cold," a reflection of the plants' alpine environment. "Pacific alpinegold" has been suggested as a standardized common name for this plant.

### Tundra hymenoxys
### *Hymenoxys grandiflora*
### (Torr. & A. Gray) K. F. Parker

The common name "hymenoxys" is generally used for this hardy plant, at home on alpine tundra. It is a true survivor whose stems and leaves are covered with dense hair, a property responsible for another common name, "old-man-of-the mountain." The hairy covering, as with that of animals, conserves metabolic heat—important for a plant that grows where temperatures often fall to well below freezing during the growing season. Given its alpine surroundings, its large flowerhead, and plump central disk, it will be recognized immediately. Its range is restricted to the northern Rocky Mountain states of Colorado, Utah, Idaho, Wyoming and Montana. (The white clustered plants in this illustration are spreading phlox, *Phlox diffusa.*)

### Stemless hymenoxys
**Hymenoxys acaulis (Pursh) Greene**

The stemless hymenoxys is less well known than its alpine relative, although the flowerheads, one to a stem, with large central disks, suggests a kinship. This is a variable plant—five varieties have been described; two grow in Idaho (the plant illustrated seems to be var. *acaulis*). Its rays are wide and their number varies; occasionally the plants are rayless. They prefer rocky ground and grow, as one or another variety throughout the West from Alberta, east to Kansas and the Dakotas, west to Nevada and California, and as far south as Texas.

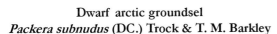

### Dwarf arctic groundsel
**Packera subnudus (DC.) Trock & T. M. Barkley**

This little ragwort (sometimes classified as *Senecio cymbalaria*) is a late-blooming alpine plant, whose prostrate configuration is typical of many alpine plants. Tiny toothed leaves and few-rayed flowerheads help with identification. It occurs in British Columbia, Alberta and south to California and Nevada. The species name, *subnudus*, refers to a relatively long, nearly leafless stem (not well shown in the illustration).

### Rocky alpine groundsel
**Packera werneriifolia (A. Gray) W. A. Weber & A. Löve**

This little plant, quite at home on alpine tundra, was classified as a *Senecio* until recently. The flowerhead is rayed, although the rays are extremely small. Its ovoid gray-green leaves and purplish involucres help to identify the plant. It is found in all of our Rocky Mountain states, and west to Arizona and California. The generic name honors botanist John G. Packer (1929- ) of the University of Alberta.

### Slender tarweed
### *Madia gracilis*
### (Sm.) D. D. Keck (left)

Tarweeds are named for their aromatic tar-like odor; this, and their twice notched rays help to identify them. The slender tarweed is found in most of our western states and in Chile—in fact, the generic name, *madia*, was derived from the plant's Chilean name, *madi*.

### Mountain tarweed (right)
### *Madia glomerata* Hook.

This odd little subalpine plant's flowerheads have small clusters of irregular ray flowers and, as here, variably large disk flowers. The hairy flower parts exude drops of sticky fluid that have a strong tar-like odor. The plants grow throughout the West to Alaska and across Canada.

### Tall ragweed (left)
### *Senecio serra* Hook.

The tall ragweed (or butterweed groundsel) is a common western meadow plant that blooms in early summer. Many small ray flowers are gathered into clusters. The species name, *serra* ("saw"), refers to its stemless, serrated leaves. The arrowleaf ragwort, *Senecio triangularis*, is an almost identical plant except for its wider, triangular-shaped leaves.

### Ballhead groundsel (right)
### *Senecio sphaerocephalus* Greene

This plant is one of the earliest blooming composites. Black-tipped bracts below the flowerhead are a distinguishing feature as are its rounded flower clusters—its species name, *sphaerocephalus*, means "round-head." It occurs in Idaho, Montana, Wyoming, Utah and Nevada.

### Stemless goldenweed
### *Stenotus acaulis* (Nutt.) Nutt.

Although the stemless goldenweed was included in the genus *Haplopappus* for many decades, it has recently been returned to Thomas Nuttall's original classification. He apparently derived the generic name *Stenotus* from the Greek *stenos,* a word that means "narrow," presumably for the shape of its leaves. Its species name, *acaulis,* means "without a stem," referring to the leaves. The plant grows in Idaho, Montana, Oregon Colorado and south to California, from foothills to alpine tundra where this plant was photographed.

### Woolly goldenweed
### *Stenotus lanuginosus* (A. Gray) Greene
### var. *andersonii* (Rydb.) C. A. Morse

The woolly goldenweed (formerly *Haplopappus lanuginosus* var. *andersonii*) is commonly seen growing in our mountains from montane to the subalpine zones, typically preferring rocky or gravelly soil. It is characterized by basally clustered, soft, narrow and rather hairy leaves. The showy flowerhead has a prominent disk and wide, deep-yellow rays.It occurs in Idaho, Washington, Oregon and Nevada. A variant, var. *lanuginosus*, occurs in southwestern Idaho, central Washington, north-eastern California and northwestern Nevada.

### Yellow mule's-ears (left)
### *Wyethia amplexicaulis* (Nutt.) Nutt.

The yellow mule's-ears (left) bears some resemblance to the arrowleaf balsamroot (page 35). Both are large plants with showy blooms although this one prefers wet meadows rather than dry hillsides. Unlike the balsamroot, it has stemless leaves (*amplexicauli*s means "stem-clasping"). Further, its leaves are shiny, sometimes described as having a varnished appearance. Yellow mules-ears bloom in the spring, usually a week or so after the white mules-ears shown below. Boston businessman Nathaniel Wyeth (1802–1856) collected both wyethias (and other plants as well) for botanist Thomas Nuttall, while in today's western Montana in 1833. The two species of Wyethia shown here grow only in Idaho and neighboring states.

Interestingly, when white and yellow wyethias grow side-by-side they may hybridize as a pale yellow-flowered form, *Wyethia* x *cusickii* Piper (upper right).

### White mule's-ears (left)
### *Wyethia helianthoides* Nutt.

This species name, *helianthoides*, means "sunflower-like"—which seems strange, as one would think that the yellow mule's-ears would have been given that name. Showy, large, spring-blooming, white wyethias are found along seasonal streams and in moist meadows, often in vast numbers. Massed wyethias in bloom are a striking sight and an irresistable subject for photographers.

### Prickly lettuce (left)
### *Lactuca serriola* L.

The prickly lettuce is a common Eurasian weed now found almost everywhere, growing on disturbed ground. It blooms from mid- to late summer. The plant's insipid-yellow flowerhead lacks disk flowers. Prickly, lobular leaves grasp a woody stem with small "ears." Prominently pointed buds and milky sap confirm its identification. *Lactuca serriola* is believed to be the ancestor of our edible lettuce, *Lactuca sativa.*

### Blue lettuce (left)
### *Mulgedium oblongifolium*
### (Nutt.) Reveal

This blue lettuce (formerly *Lactuca pulchella*) is the showiest of our several native wild lettuces. Despite its attractive flower-head, it is considered a weed. Its leaves, growth habit and distribution are similar to those of the prickly lettuce.

Jane Lundin

### Yellow salsify (above right)
### *Tragopogon dubius* Scop.

As its name, *dubius,* suggests, the yellow salsify is part of a confusingly interbred genus, one that includes the very similar, blue-flowered salsify, *Tragopogon porrifolius,* also known as the "oyster plant." Both were introduced from the Old World for their edible roots (although this plant's stringy roots would hardly seem edible). They now grow almost everywhere in the United States excepting the deep south. *Tragopogon* means "goat's beard," from the plant's large, dandelion-like, feathery seed head.

### Common tansy
### *Tanacetum vulgare* L.

Tansy is a Eurasian perennial that now grows everywhere in the Northern Hemisphere. It is sometimes seen in Idaho at higher elevations, always near settled places. The tansy's button-like flowers, and camphor-like odor are unique so there will be no problem with identification. Not only is the plant ornamental, but it is also an effective vermifuge. Tansy teas and extracts were used medicinally for other conditions, although with some risk and questionable benefit. Tansies also contain the insect repellant pyrethrum and their leaves were formerly used to wrap meat to prevent spoiling, and added to winding sheets to deter worms, supposedly explaining the derivation of *Tanacetum* (and "tansy") from the Greek *athanasia*, a word that means "no death," i.e., "immortal."

### Pineapple weed
### *Matricaria discoidea* DC

Meriwether Lewis found specimens of this plant, native to Idaho, growing along the Clearwater River on June 12, 1806. He described it as "a small plant of an agreeable sweet scent; flowers yellow." The crushed plant gives off an odor close to that of a pineapple, explaining its common name. Related to the European plant used to make camomile tea, ours has been used for the same purpose. It is a common, non-aggressive garden and border weed found in almost every state and province. The pineapple weed grows in our mountains on disturbed ground to mid-elevations where it blooms from mid-summer on. The name *Matricaria* is said to imply "mother-care" for the plants' supposed value in treating uterine conditions.

### Large-flowered brickellia
### *Brickellia grandiflora*
### (Hook.) Nutt.

The brickellias are plain cousins of the showier joe pye-weeds (*Eupatorium* spp.); they are not plants that one would collect for an ornamental garden. You will see them growing at high elevations in our mountains and at lower elevations elsewhere, west of the Mississippi River. The plants' pale yellow to white flowerheads lack rays and appear to be squeezed together and held in place by the involucral bracts. Prominent delta-shaped leaves also help to identify this species. The plants bloom late, from mid-summer on. The genus name, *Brickellia*, honors botanist and physician, John Brickell (1748-1809) of Savannah, Georgia. Several similar species of *Brickellia* are also native to Idaho.

### Western snakeroot
### *Ageratina occidentalis*
### (Hook.) R. M. King & H. E. Rob.

This plant, also known as the western boneset, was until recently classified as a *Eupatorium,* a genus that includes the common joe pye-weeds This, and species shown on neighboring pages, are rayless composites. Protruding forked styles, a distinguishing feature of composites in general, give the flowers a feathery appearance. The western boneset is relatively uncommon, favoring subalpine to alpine cliffs and other rocky surroundings. The name *Ageratina* was that of a unknown ancient Greek plant, and means "everlasting," from the suffix *a* for "not" and *gera* for "old" (for its long-lasting flowers). David Douglas collected this species on the "Lewis and Clark River" (today's Snake River).

### Dusty maiden
### *Chaenactis douglasii*
### (Hook.) Hook. & Arn.
### var. *douglasii*

The generic name *Chaenactis* was derived from the Greek *chaino* meaning "to gape" and *aktin* meaning "ray," for the wide-mouthed flowers on the periphery of the disk are wide-mouthed. One might not recognize this frilly-leaved plant as an Asteraceae, but the protruding forked styles are a tipoff. The florets are white to pale pink, their color accentuated by the pink styles. The dusty maiden grows to fairly high elevations, and blooms—often in great numbers—on dry slopes. Dull gray-green ("glaucous"), frilly leaves explain the common name, "dusty maiden." Another species, *Chaenactis evermannii* Greene, seen at higher altitudes, has similar leaves but its flowerheads are markedly wooly.

### Alpine chaenactis
### *Chaenactis douglasii*
### (Hook.) Hook. & Arn.
### var. *alpina* A. Gray

The alpine chaenactis is a small perennial that blooms toward summer's end, nestled among the rocks of talus slopes near treeline and above. It resembles a smaller version of *Chaenactis douglasii* var. *douglasii,* differing in its white flowerheads and bare stems. The differences between the two plants were formerly deemed sufficient to allow each its own species designation; now, however, they are classified as varieties of the same species. Darwin would have been pleased to see how the two plants have evolved in different ecological settings from a common ancestral form. While this plant is restricted to Idaho and surrounding states (less Washington and Nevada), var. *douglasii* is widespread in the Far West.

### Rosy pussy-toes (left)
### *Antennaria rosea* Greene

Pussy-toes are not particularly attractive, but they are so numerous that one cannot help but notice them—this one especially, for its reddish hue. A rosette of basal leaves gives off a stem surmounted by a cluster of small flowerheads about the size of a house-cat's digital pad, whence their common name. After the "toes" open one can see that each flowerhead is made up of many tiny flowers. There are several varieties of *Antennaria rosea*—we will not attempt to identify this one further. The name *Antennaria* was apparently derived from the resemblance of the flower's pappus to an insect antenna.

### Rocky Mountain pussy-toes
### *Antennaria media* Greene
### (below left)

The Rocky Mountain pussy-toes, shown here in flower, grows on alpine and arctic tundra in our western mountain states and provinces, north to Alaska, and south to California, Arizona and New Mexico. Its tiny oval leaves are covered with fine hairs giving them a color more gray than green. It is commmonly found on rocky ground where it is nurtured by the retained heat of the sun.

### *Antennaria* sp. (right)

The photo shows the typical appearance of grouped pussy-toes (probably *Antennaria umbrinella* Rydb.). There are many antennarias; the two species shown on the left are not hard to identify, but others require an appropriate reference source for help with their classification.

### Pearly-everlasting (above)
### *Anaphalis margaritacea*
### (L.) Benth. & Hook. f.

*Anaphalis* is the ancient Greek name for a similar plant. The name *margaritacea* echoes its common name, "pearly." Each of its round, white flowerheads has a characteristic diffuse black dot on the surrounding involucre. The only member of the genus, it is related to *Antennaria* and grows in most of North America. It is often used in dried flower arrangements. Supposedly the pearly-everlasting was the first North American herb to be cultivated in Europe, because of purported medicinal value.

### Hooker's thistle
### *Cirsium hookerianum* Nutt. (left)

Hooker's, or white thistle, was given the name *hookerianum* by Thomas Nuttall in 1841 to honor William Jackson Hooker (1785-1865), professor of botany at Glasgow and later Director of England's Royal Botanic Garden. The plant grows at high elevations in the coastal ranges of British Columbia, the Cascade Range in Washington and in the Rocky Mountains states of Idaho, Montana and Wyoming. Its white flowerhead makes identication easy. *Cirsium* is a Greek word for a knot of veins, a condition that thistles were used to treat in the distant past.

### Elk thistle
### *Cirsium foliosum* (Hook.) DC. (below left)

The elk thistle blooms in early summer along mountain streams and in wet meadows. The young plants are eaten by elk and bears; the peeled stems are edible for humans. The plants are easily identified by their size (it is our largest native thistle), by its many prickly pinnate leaves (*foliosum* means "leafy"), and by bracts (specialized leaves that cup the flower parts) that extend well above a pinkish flower-head that turns brown as the plant matures. Both this plant and Hooker's thistle were gathered by Thomas Drummond (1780-1835), a Scot who collected plants in western America.

### Jackson Hole thistle
### *Cirsium inamoenum* (Greene) D. J. Keil  (below)

The Jackson Hole thistle (*Cirsium subniveum* is an earlier scientific name) grows along roads and trails, blooming in mid-summer. The plants have a bush-like appearance, growing year after year in the same location. They have hard, serrated, spiny leaves, and pale pinkish or lavender thistle-like flowers, borne on branching stems. It grows in Idaho and contiguous states (excepting Washington) as well as in California.

**Spotted knapweed**
*Centaurea stoebe* L.

**Cornflower**
*Centaurea cyanus* L.

The spotted knapweed (previously *Centaurea maculosa* and *Centaurea biebersteinii*) is an import from southwestern Europe that has spread throughout the United States (including Hawaii), Canada and Mexico. There are other similar species of knapweeds, but this one is the most troublesome. Many places in Idaho, as high as the montane zone, are purple with blooming knapweed by mid-summer. As with many weeds, its flower is attractive, with three-parted rays. It can be identified by its straggly appearance, its purple flowers and the spotted involucre below the flower parts. It has recently been shown—as long suspected—that the roots of knapweed release a plant poison that aids in its spread. Biologists are studying the possibility of controlling the plant, using insects imported from its Old World environment.

The cornflower (also bachelor's button) is, as its appearance suggests, related to the knapweed. The plant, a favorite ornamental, has escaped and established itself as a foothill plant in Idaho and elsewhere in the United States. It is a much-loved wildflower in Europe, where it is the national flower of Poland. For the present, at least, it seems to grow as a non-aggressive weed in North America.

**Canadian thistle (left)**
*Cirsium arvense* (L.) Scop.

The Canadian thistle, like the spotted knapweed, is a noxious, spreading, exotic plant, originally a native of Eurasia, but now found in all but our southernmost states, and in all the Canadian provinces. It is a truly serious weed, one that is not easily missed, for it grows tall, with deep purple flowers. It is a deeply rooted, perennial plant that—like the knapweed—is difficult to eradicate. It is commonly seen growing on disturbed ground, usually along roads and railroads. Recently, however, we have seen it growing high in the montane zone, well away from a populated area.

### Common yarrow
### *Achillea millefolium* L.

The common yarrow is a circumboreal plant that resembles members of the carrot family—look closely, however, and you'll see that each "flower" has, in addition to wide little ray flowers, a disk made up of tiny florets. The yarrow is a survivor; it grows all through the Northern Hemisphere from sea level to alpine tundra, blooming from late spring into the fall. The name *Achillea* comes from the belief that Achilles used yarrows to treat his companion's wounds. Like many of the Asteraceae, it has an aromatic, medicinal odor. This plant and its relatives have been used medicinally for millenia by many cultures, although it has no scientifically proven therapeutic value. The species name, *millefolium*, describes the plant's finely divided leaves. As with many widely distributed species, there are many—a dozen or so—varieties. Lewis and Clark collected the common yarrow on May 20, 1806, in today's northern Idaho.

### Louisiana sage
### *Artemisia ludoviciana* Nutt.
### var. *incompta* (Nutt.) Cronquist

Next to the big sage (our common sagebrush), the Louisiana sage (also known as prairie sage and western mugwort) is the species of *Artemisia* most commonly encountered in Idaho. It grows almost everywhere in the United States and Canada. Several varieties are recognized; the one shown here is not often seen for it is an alpine plant. Its leaves are more divided, less pubescent (covered with fine hair), and greener than the common var. *latiloba* that grows at lower altitudes. Louisiana sage, in common with other artemisias, has a strong herbal odor, helpful in identifying members of this genus.

# Barberry Family (Berberidaceae)

The Barberry family consists of 13 genera and 660 species. While most are in the north temperate zone, others are scattered throughout the world in what appears to be a haphazard fashion, suggesting—along with certain plant characteristics—that they are among the less specialized of the angiosperms (flowering plants). The various genera are quite disparate—the best known native North American species are the eastern mayapple (*Podophyllum peltatum*) from which the anti-tumor medication podophyllin is obtained and, in the West, the several species of Oregon grape (species of *Berberis*). The common barberry (*Berberis vulgaris*), a red-berried hedge-plant, is a native of Europe. Several other barberries, e.g., the Japanese barberry (*Berberis thunbergii*) as well as the Oregon grapes are used as ornamentals in hedges and as ground-cover, the family's main economic importance. Most are woody, sometimes brambly, shrubs. Some are evergreen. The flowers have four to six sepals and the same number of petals, although, because they are joined, the petals can be hard to count. The origin of the word "berberis," from which "barberry" was derived, is unknown, but its usage goes back at least to the 15th century. Apparently the resemblance to "berry" is fortuitous.

### Creeping Oregon grape
### *Berberis repens* Lindl.

The creeping Oregon, or holly, grape grows in open woods where it spreads by woody rhizomes (*repens* means "creeping"). Deep green to rusty-red holly-like leaves, and distinctive flowers and fruit, make it easy to identify. Blue berries appear in mid- to late summer and, while edible, are best used for preserves. The plant grows in all of the western states and provinces, as well as in scattered locations further east. It is sometimes also classified as *Mahonia repens*, honoring Irish-born Philadelphia horticulturist Bernard M'Mahon (1775-1816). M'Mahon had access to Lewis and Clark's plant specimens and grew this plant from their seeds, probably ones collected in northern Idaho in 1805 or 1806.*

---

*The explorers brought back specimens of two other Oregon grapes—shiny-leaved *Berberis aquifolium* and dull-leaved *Berberis nervosa*, collected at todays The Dalles in Oregon; both plants, unlike the creeping Oregon grape, are bushes, often used in landscape gardening. Their flowers and fruit are similar to those shown here. These plants also grow in Idaho, but *Berberis repens* is the species found in our mountains.

## Borage (Forget-me-not) Family (Boraginaceae)

The Borage family's name was derived from an attractive, blue-flowered European plant, *Borago officinalis*, found in the United States only as an imported ornamental. Its name possibly comes from the Latin *burra*, meaning a "rough garment" or "coat," referring to the plant's hairy leaves and stem. As borage is unfamiliar to most Americans, "forget-me-not" is often used as the family common name. There are 117 genera and 2,435 species in the family; ninety or so species grow in the American Northwest. Many look so much alike that identification of individual plants can be difficult, depending more on seed ("nutlet") properties than on plant appearance. Family characteristics include: alternate bristly leaves and loose clumps of flowers borne on a stem that in some species seems to unroll (i.e., they're "scorpioid") as the flowers open. The flowers, typically blue, but sometimes white, pink or yellow, are radially symmetrical. Five petals (occasionally four) are joined at the base to form a tube. The ovary is four-parted; each part forms one nutlet or seed. In some species the nutlets have barbed spines that stick to the fur of passing animals and to hikers' socks and shoelaces, explaining why "stickseed" is a common name for the plants. Most of the Boraginaceae are herbaceous (i.e., non-woody). Some are used as ornamental plants, the family's chief economic importance. These include species of *Myosotis* (forget-me-nots), *Heliotropium* (heliotropes), *Mertensia* (bluebells), and others.

### Meadow forget-me-not
### *Hackelia micrantha*
### (Eastw.) J. L. Gentry

Many different "forget-me-nots" grow in Idaho. The one pictured here, considerably magnified, is variously known as the small-flowered (or false) forget-me-not, blue stickseed, or simply as a hackelia. Hikers often encounter hackelias, for their seeds cling tenaciously to clothing. The plants grow at least as high as treeline, blooming in late spring or early summer. They may be two or more feet tall, and have stout-stems with furry, lanceolate leaves. Their small flowers are borne in loose clumps; their petals have a small raised fold at the base. Sometimes there are so many as to form blue patches on mountain slopes. While the flowers are usually blue, occasionally they are white or pink. The species ranges from British Columbia and Alberta, south to California, Nevada, Utah and Colorado. The name *Hackelia* honors Czech botanist Joseph Hackel (1783-1869).

### Spreading stickseed
### *Hackelia patens* (Nutt.) I. M. Johnst.

The spreading (also spotted) stickseed has the five-petaled flowers typical of those seen in the genus *Hackelia* and in several other genera whose members are also commonly called "wild forget-me-nots." Other than having white flowers (sometimes, as here, with bluish markings), the plant is similar to the hackelia shown above, although less widely distributed. Spreading stickseeds are found in Idaho (where they are common), Montana, Wyoming, Utah, and Nevada.

Arctic alpine forget-me-not
*Eritrichium nanum* (Villars) Schrader

This forget-me-not is a striking little alpine plant whose bright blue blossoms stand out vividly against drab mountain tundra. The plants form matted "cushions" made up of tiny, tightly clustered leaves. This lovely little plant was photographed above treeline in our White Cloud Range. It grows in the Rocky Mountains as far south as New Mexico, in Alaska, and in mountain ranges of Europe and Asia.

Asian forget-me-not
*Myosotis asiatica* (Vesterg.) Schischk. & Serg.

The Asian forget-me-not is a circumboreal plant that prefers moist subalpine and alpine meadows. It grows in our Northwest, south to Colorado, and north to Alaska. Its small, five-petaled, bright blue flowers, similar to those of other forget-me-nots, and wide lanceolate leaves identify the plant. *Myosotis* was derived from two Greek words meaning "mouse-ear," used in the past for a now unknown plant. Plants in this genus are considered to be the true forget-me-nots.

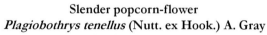

Slender popcorn-flower
*Plagiobothrys tenellus* (Nutt. ex Hook.) A. Gray

Several genera in the borage family are made up of very small plants. This plant's flowers are only about an eighth of an inch in diameter and the plant may stand no more than three inches high. The leaves and stem are hairy, a clue to placing it in the Borage family. Its range extends from British Columbia, south to Baja California, and east to Idaho, Utah and Arizona. Meriwether Lewis was botanizing at The Dalles, in present day Oregon, on April 17, 1806, while his men were portaging around the Narrows of the Columbia River and he collected a specimen of the slender popcorn-flower there. Frederick Pursh apparently overlooked Lewis's specimen when he classified the expedition's flora and it remained for others to find and describe it decades later. The name *Plagiobothrys* was derived from two Greek words and means "obliquely pitted" referring to the appearance of the plant's nutlet. The species name, *tenellus*, is Latin for "slender."

### Waterton Lakes cryptantha
### *Cryptantha sobolifera* Payson

The genus *Cryptantha* is a large one that includes about forty species, all grow west of the Mississippi River, and approximately fifteen species are found in Idaho. Nevertheless, cryptanthas seem not to be common in our mountains as many grow only at lower elevations. The plant shown here, also known as the alpine cryptantha (or alpine cat's eye) is an exception for it is a true alpine plant. In common with other plants in the genus, it is small, only one to five inches high. Its leaves, stems, and calyces are notably bristly and its tiny, clustered, five-petaled white flowers are borne on relatively long stems that arise from a basal gathering of lanceolate leaves. Because the plant is listed as being native only to Idaho, Montana, Nevada and mountains of Oregon and California, one wonders how it came by its common name, for the Waterton Lakes National Park is in Alberta, contiguous with our Glacier National Park. The species name, *sobolifera,* derived from the Latin, means "sobole-bearing."( A "sobole" is a shoot or sprout—i.e., a sucker—that grows at the base of a plant.) *Cryptantha* is a taxonomically confusing genus; this plant has had several species names including *Cryptantha hypsophila* and *Cryptantha nubigena* (the latter name is now relegated to a separate species that grows only in California).

### Alpine bluebell
### *Mertensia alpina* (Torr.) G. Don

The alpine bluebell, in common with many alpine plants, is small, only four or five inches high. It has a localized distribution, found only in Idaho, Montana, Wyoming, Colorado, and in New Mexico where it is rare. It is also uncommon in Idaho, apparently found only in higher mountains close to the Idaho-Montana border (Fremont County). It is an attractive little plant that may be recognizd by its small size, flaring petals and by its presence on alpine tundra.

### Ciliate bluebell
### *Mertensia ciliata*
### (James ex Torr.) G. Don

The ciliate (or mountain) bluebell's species name, *ciliata*, means "fringed" for the fine hairs that can be seen along the edges of back-lighted leaves. The plants grow nearly to tree-line in moist meadows and along streambanks, often forming "rivers" of green and blue. When shaded, the flowers are deep blue and a lighter color when growing in full sunlight. The plants are two to three feet tall, and bare lush, elliptical to broadly lanceolate leaves. Mountain bluebells are a favorite browse plant for elk and deer, and it is common to find matted areas where large animals have bedded down, sometimes to give birth to their young, in the thick plant growth. The ciliate bluebell grows in all of the Rocky Mountain states.

### Idaho bluebell
### *Mertensia campanulata* A. Nelson

The Idaho bluebell is found only in central Idaho. A tall meadow plant, it often grows in profusion in well circumscribed areas. The leaves, stems and flowers all have a pronounced frosted ("glaucous") appearance; the smooth leaves lack prominent veins. Idaho bluebells flower in late spring and then, with the summer's heat, the plants disappear. For whatever reason, they may not reappear in the same location in subsequent years. The word *campanulata* means "bell-shaped," a term that could equally well be applied to the flowers of most mertensias. The common name "bluebell" is used for many other, quite unrelated, plants emphasizing the importance of binomial scientific names.

### Oregon bluebell
### *Mertensia bella* Piper

The Oregon bluebell is the least common of the several species of mertensia shown here, for, while it occurs in Idaho, Montana, Oregon and California, it is considered to be an uncommon plant in all four states; it is found only in Clearwater and Idaho counties in Idaho. It may be identified by thin, green leaves. Their upper surface is covered with fine hairs, the undersurface is smooth. The leaves' veins are more prominent than those of our other mertensias. The flowers are open and the small lobes at the end are rounded. The plant is usually found in moist surroundings, growing to mid-elevations in our mountains.

### Leafy bluebell
### *Mertensia oblongifolia* (Nutt.) G. Don

The leafy bluebell is one of our earliest spring wildflowers, blooming on sagebrush-covered slopes soon after snowmelt. The name, *"oblongifolia,"* describes the plant's wide leaves. All mertensias have five sepals enclosing five petals. These form a tube that flares more or less abruptly. Rarely, one sees an albino form of this plant. Eighteen species of *Mertensia* grow in North America, this plant is restricted to our western states. German botanist Karl Heinrich Merten (1796-1830) collected the plant while on a Russian scientific expedition to Alaska in 1827. The genus *Mertensia* was named in honor of his father, Franz Karl Merten (1764–1831), also a botanist.

### Columbia puccoon
### *Lithospermum ruderale* Douglas ex Lehm.

The Columbia puccoon (members of this genus are also known as gromwells or stoneseeds) is a western plant ranging north to Alberta and British Columbia, south through the Rocky Mountain states to Colorado, Utah and Nevada and west to the three coastal states. It is a moderately tall plant with prominently ribbed leaves. The leaves and stems are coated with fine hairs giving the plants an overall grayish-green appearance. Its seeds (nutlets) are bony hard, explaining its scientific name *Lithospermum* ("stone-seed," derived from the Latin). The species name, *ruderale*, also Latin, means "dump" or "waste-place," although the plant is no more commonly found in disturbed areas than are many other wildflowers.

Seeds of the European *Lithospermum officinale*, and possibly of ours as well, were used medicinally in times past to treat bladder stones in the belief that "like cures like." The roots of the Columbia puccoon contain a yellow dye used by Native Americans. The roots of the related eastern plant, *Lithospermum canescens,* contain a red dye. Captain John Smith wrote in 1612: "Pocones is a small roote that groweth in the mountaines, which being dryed and beate in powder turneth red" and used by the Indians to paint their skin. Smith's observation may have been the origin of the term "redskin."

### Common fiddleneck
### *Amsinckia menziesii*
### (Lehm.) A. Nelson & J. F. Macbr.

The common (also "small-flowered") fiddleneck is a widely distributed native weed, growing to subalpine elevations. In common with many Boraginaceae it has bristly stems, leaves, and flower parts. The flowers bloom on an unrolling stem known botanically as a "helicoid" or "scorpioid cyme," from which the name "fiddleneck" was derived. The plants sometimes grow in such numbers as to turn fields yellow. Livestock avoid the stiffly bristled plants, so the fiddleneck is classified as a troublesome weed. The plant was first described by German botanist Johann Georg Christian Lehmann (1792–1860), who gave it the generic name *Amsinckia* to honor a 19th c. benefactor of the Hamburg Botanical Garden, William Amsinck. Lewis and Clark collected this species on the Columbia in 1806, although Archibald Menzies, (1754-1842)*, surgeon and botanist with the Vancouver Expedition (1791-1795), had found it earlier, explaining its present species name.

---

*Menzies made the first ascent of Hawaii's Mauna Loa in 1794 accompanied by two companions. He, measuried the mountain's height quite accurately with an anaeroid barometer.

# Boraginaceae

## German madwort
### *Asperugo procumbens* L.

German madwort, or catchweed, is a field weed that grows to mid-elevations in our mountains. It is one of several introduced plants in the borage family that have spread throughout the United States and Canada. Others include the viper's bugloss (*Echium vulgare*, not shown) and species of hounds-tongues. These are serious weeds in some parts of the United States, but the German madwort is a relatively non-aggressive plant. So far as we can determine, it has no value as a food or browse plant, although in times past it was used—ineffectually, we presume—to treat rabies, thus the name "madwort."

## Common hound's-tongue
### *Cynoglossum officinale* L.

The common hound's-tongue may grow to high montane elevations in our mountains, and seems to be spreading farther and farther away from human settlements. It was introduced to the New World from Europe, most likely as both a medicinal and ornamental plant. Unless one knows the plant, it can be difficult to identify, for it is usually not included in wild-flower guides. It may grow to be three feet or more tall with narrow gray-green furry leaves and many clustered, showy, dark-red to purple flowers. *Cynoglossum officinale* is now found in much of North America, and in all but a few of our southern states. The plant can spread aggressively and is considered a noxious weed in Washington, Wyoming and Colorado. Several other species of hound's-tongues are native to the United States, but none are found in Idaho.

In common with many plants with the species name *officinale* ("of the shop"; pharmacy shop implied), the common hound's-tongue has been used medicinally for various purposes in the past, chiefly as a healing poultice. The name "hound's-tongue," the translation of both Latin and Greek names for the plant, has been used in English for a millenium and more.

## Cabbage, or Mustard Family (Brassicaceae)

The scientific family name Brassicaceae is derived from the Latin *brassica*, a word that means "cabbage." (An older family name, Cruciferae, is still in use although most botanists prefer the former name.) The family contains many valuable food plants rich in vitamin C and sulfur compounds—the latter are responsible for the typical smell and taste of foods such as cabbage, brussel sprouts, broccoli, turnip, and mustard (all of which belong to the genus *Brassica*), water cress (*Rorippa* spp.), radishes (*Raphanus* spp.), and many others. While these are of great economic importance, the family also contributes ornamentals to our gardens: ornamental cabbages, wall-flowers (*Erysimum* spp.), rockcresses (*Arabis* spp.), and others. The flowers' four petals usually form a cross, explaining the older family name Cruciferae, derived from the Latin *crus* (cross) and *fero* (I bear) and members of the family are often referred to as "crucifers."

The flowers are frequently borne in clusters ("racemes"). Leaves are usually simple, alternate, and lack a petiole (a leaf stem). Most of the Brassicaceae form seedpods. When these are long, they are "siliques"; when short, they are known as "silicles." The leaves and other parts of the plants often have a radishy taste. Members are represented in our mountains by several genera and many species, including some with showy flowers, as shown on the following pages. Most likely any small, four-petaled, early spring-blooming wildflower will belong to the mustard family, although further identification can be difficult for there are many similar species. Recent changes in classification have also made identifying plants in this family more difficult.

## Cusick's rockcress
### *Boechera cusickii*
### (S. Watson) Al-Shebaz

Cusick's rockcress (formerly *Arabis cusickii* S. Watson ) grows only in Idaho, Nevada, Washington and Oregon. Its flowers range from purple to nearly white. The plant may be identified by its crowded flower cluster, leafy stems and pendulous fruiting bodies or "siliques" (not present in the illustration). Its silvery-green color comes from fine hairs that cover the foliage. William Conklin Cusick (1842-1942) was an Oregon school-teacher, rancher, and botanist who collected and described many plants native to Oregon's mountains.

## Hoary rockcress,
### *Boechera puberula*
### (Nutt.) Dorn

The chances are that any pink-to-purple, spring-blooming, four-petaled plant found in our mountains will be a *Boechera*. This showy little plant's species name, *puberula,* implies that its gray-green leaves are covered with minute hairs. It grows in Idaho, in the three Pacific coastal states, Utah and Nevada. Many rockcresses prefer rocky ground explaining their common name. The generic name *Boechera* honors Danish botanist Tyge W. Böcher (1909-1983).

### Holboell's rockcress
### *Boechera holboellii*
### (Hornem.) A. Löve & D. Löve

Holboell's rockcress is widely distributed. It is found in the West, Midwest, east to Quebec and north to Alaska and Greenland. As is common with plants having a wide range, many varieties are recognized; several occur in Idaho—the plant shown here is var. *secunda* (Howell) Dorn. Holboell's rockcress may be identified at the species level by its pendulous siliques. It is encountered fairly frequently, growing as high as the subalpine zone.

The species name, *holboellii,* honors an eminent Danish naturalist, Carl Peter Holboell (1795-1856), a man whose interests apparently varied greatly, for various species of birds, molluscs and fish also bear his name.

### Wind River rockcress
### *Boechera williamsii* (Rollins) Dorn
### var. *saximontana* (Rollins) Dorn

This recently reclassified plant appears to be William's rockcress (identified as *Arabis microphylla* var. *saximontana* in the first edition of this book). It is an uncommon, tiny plant characterized by smooth-surfaced basal leaves, few-leaved stems and small clusters of attractive pink-to-purple four-petaled flowers. Look for it shortly after snowmelt, close to treeline. Two varieties are recognized. One, var. *williamsii,* is found only in Wyoming where the species was first collected. The other, this plant, grows in Idaho, Wyoming, and Montana.

### Nuttall's rockcress
### *Arabis nuttallii* (Kuntze) B. L. Rob.

Nuttall's rockcress is at home from foothills to mid-montane elevations. A thin stem arises from a basal rosette of leaves, topped by a cluster of white to pinkish flowers that form upward pointing siliques.

Englishman Thomas Nuttall (1786-1859), generally accepted as the greatest of our early botanists, spent years botanizing in the United States and western North America. His *Genera of North American Plants* appeared in 1818 and led to an appointment as Curator of Harvard's Botanic Garden, a post he held for more than a decade. Then, following a productive overland trip to the Pacific coast, he returned to England and lived there for the remainder of his life.

**Alpine bladderpod**
***Physaria reediana*** O'Kane & Al-Shehbaz

The alpine bladderpod, formerly *Lesquerella alpina* (Nutt.) S. Watson, blooms in the spring on dry subalpine ridges. The common name "bladderpod" is derived from the plants' round fruiting bodies (not obvious in the illustration). It is native to the northern Rocky Mountains, and neighboring states, growing as far north as Alberta and south to Colorado.

**Western bladderpod**
***Physaria occidentalis***
**(S. Watson) O'Kane & Al-Shehbaz**

The western bladderpod (previously *Lesquerella occidentale* S. Watson) is a small, more common plant than the alpine bladderpod shown on the left. It grows on gravelly ground from mid-elevations to subalpine slopes. Spoon-shaped leaves are unique to this species and serve to identify it, as does the centrifugal growth pattern of the clusters. It grows in Idaho, Nevada, and Utah as well as in the mountains of the three Pacific coastal states.

**Common twinpod (left)**
***Physaria didymocarpa*** (Hook.) A. Gray

The twinpod physaria is unusual as its fruit is split into two short, joined pods. Even when the plant is not fruiting, as with the plant in the illustration, it can be identified by its basal cluster of furry, gray-green, ovoid leaves and its four-petaled bright yellow flowers. This little plant is found at higher elevations in our mountains, growing on dry, gravelly ground. It grows in Idaho, Wyoming, Montana, North Dakota and Alberta (and rarely in Washington and British Columbia). The name *Physaria* is from a Greek word meaning "bladder" or "bellows" for the shape of the silicle (fruiting body). The species name, *didymocarpa*, is also from the Greek and means "twin fruit." Three varieties are recognized, the one shown here, var. *didymocarpa*, grows in Idaho.

**Few-seeded draba (left)**
*Draba oligosperma* Hook.

The species name, *oligosperma*, means "few seeds." The few-seeded draba grows in all but the most southern of our western mountain states and in Canadian provinces, from lower elevations to subalpine slopes. While its flowers are similar to other plants shown on this page, its narrow leaves do not form mats.

**Globe-fruited draba (below)**
*Draba sphaerocarpa*
**J. F. Macbr. & Payson**

Some drabas are localized to a single mountain range; this cushion-forming plant, for example, grows only on exposed alpine and subalpine ridges of the Sawtooth Mountains. Its common and species names both refer to its rounded fruit. While many draba species are quite similar, tentative identification is often possible based on plant location and morphology. Definitive identification often depends on technical differences among the fruits of various species.

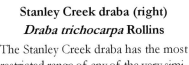

### *Draba* spp.

Made up of about 350 species, the drabas are the largest genus in the mustard family. The name, from Greek antiquity, was used for a now unknown crucifer. "Whitlow grass" is a common name because draba poultices were used in the past to treat "whitlows," or "run-arounds"—infections that form at the base of finger-nails. At lower altitudes drabas tend to be long-stemmed solitary plants with plain white, pink, or yellow flowers. At higher elevations, they form compact clumps on rocky slopes, usually flowering at the end of snowmelt.

**Payson's draba (above)**
*Draba paysonii* J. F Macbr.

Payson's draba is found only at high elevations in the Sierras, and in the northern Rocky Mountains of the United States and Canada. The plant shown here was photographed well above treeline on Mount Borah, Idaho's highest mountain. Its tiny, hairy, clustered leaves grow at ground level and remain well hidden when the plants are in flower. Two varieties are recognized; ours is var. *treleasii* (O. E. Schulz) C. L. Hitchc.

**Stanley Creek draba (right)**
*Draba trichocarpa* Rollins

The Stanley Creek draba has the most restricted range of any of the very similar alpine/subalpine plants shown on this page, for it is found only near Stanley, Idaho. Because this species was described relatively recently it is often not listed in regional plant guides. Its four-petaled flowers are small and remain partially closed, and its tiny leaves form tight clusters. The species name, *trichocarpa,* means "hairy fruit."

### Lance-leaf draba
### *Draba cana* Rydb.

The lance-leaf draba (also known as the cushion whitlow-grass) blooms later in the spring than do those shown on the previous page, favoring high open slopes and rocky crevices. This plant's classification has been a source of confusion in the past. It has variously been classified as *Draba lanceolata* or as a variety of *Draba breweri*. The classification above is correct. The plant is found throughout the Rocky Mountains to Alaska, east across the continent to several northern states, and south to California, Nevada, New Mexico, and Utah. It also grows in Greenland and Eurasia.

### Alpine smelowskia
### *Smelowskia americana* (Regel & Herder) Rydb.

The alpine smelowskia (until recently classified as *Smelowskia calycina*) is a somewhat protean plant, with hairy, variably pinnate basal leaves, three-lobed terminal leaflets, ovoid narrow-based petals and quite prominent anthers and styles. Its fruit is ovoid with a protruberant tip—a few are seen in the illustration. Alpine smelowskias prefer rocky alpine and subalpine terrain. It grows in the central and northern Rocky Mountains, north to Alaska. The name honors Timotheus Smelowski (1770-1815), a Russian botanist. "False candytuft" has been proposed as an alternate common name for smelowskias.

### Idaho candytuft
### *Noccaea fendleri* (A. Gray) Holub var. *idahoense* (Payson) F. K. Mey.

Two native thlaspis, formerly varieties of *Thlaspi fendleri*, have recently been reclassified into separate species: *Noccaea montanum* and the plant shown here (until recently classified as *Thlaspi idahoense* Payson). The two are distinguishable chiefly by the configuration of their leaves. The leaves of the former are rounder and have well developed petioles (leaf stems), whereas the leaves of the plant illustrated here, the Idaho candytuft, are more lanceolate and taper gradually to attach directly to the main stem, as seen in the illustration. Our plant grows in the mountains of central Idaho, whereas the alpine species is found in all of our western states.

The genus *Noccaea* honors Domenico Nocca (1758-1841) an Italian clergyman and botanist who was the director of the botanical garden at Pavia.

### Western tansy mustard
### *Descurainia pinnata* (Walter) Britton

*Descurainia* is a confusing genus. All members are weeds. A few are imports, but most are native plants. Ours appears to be a variety of *Descurainia pinnata*, although we will not attempt to classify it further as no less than ten varieties are recognized, based on relatively minor differences in morphology. The plant shown here is very common, growing to mid-elevations in our mountains. The species, in one variety or another, occurs throughout the United States. It is characterized by clusters of small four-petaled yellow flowers, erect siliques (just forming here) and pinnate leaves—whence the species name *pinnata*. "Pinnate tansy mustard" is another, more appropriate, common name.

Young plants are similar in appearance to those of the flixweed, (*Descurainia sophia* (L.) Webb ex Prantl, not shown) a troublesome import, that has spread all across North America. As the flixweed matures it develops frizzy, bi- or tri-pinnate leaves, distinguishing it from native species. The genus *Descurainia* was named for French botanist François Descurain (1658-1740).

### Western wallflower
### *Erysimum asperum* (Nutt.) DC. var. *elatum* (Nutt.) Torr.*

Half a dozen varieties of western wallflower are recognized. Ours is found in Idaho, Utah and Nevada. It grows on rocky slopes—often on talus—at mid- to subalpine elevations. Its growth habit and its large, showy, yellow-orange flowerheads identify this attractive plant. After the petals fall away, its flowers form "siliques," slim seed-containing pods. The generic name, *Erysimum*, was used by the Greeks for a related plant. Lewis and Clark collected the western wallflower while camped near present-day Kamiah, Idaho, on 1 June, 1806.

The species name, *asperum*, means "rough," but we don't know why it was used for this plant, whereas the varietal name "*elatum*" (tall) is quite suitable.

---

*This plant is a member of a group of very similar plants about which there is taxonomic debate; we have chosen to use the classification above. The plant is also known as Pursh's wallflower and then may be classified as *Erysimum capitatum* (Douglas ex Hook.) Greene var *purshii* (Durand) Rollins.

### Wormseed mustard
### *Erysimum cheiranthoides* L.

A wetland plant, the wormseed mustard (also wormseed wallflower, treacle mustard), and the watercress shown below have much the same distribution; both are found in most of the United States and all of the Canadian provinces. This plant prefers moist places and is usually seen with its roots in water; it is at home at least as high as the montane zone. The flowerheads are similar to those of other erysimums, supported by thick stems that bear alternating leaves ranging in shape from lanceolate to ovoid. Its siliques are long and thin and the crushed seeds apparently are an effective treatment for intestinal worms. The latter property explains the "wormseed" in its common names. A common plant in Eurasia, it is considered an exotic in North America. The species name, *cheiranthoides*, means "like a *cheiranthus*," an older term for genus *Erysimum*. The word *cheiranthus*, in turn, was derived from two Greek words meaning "red-flower," an old name for some species of mustard plant.

### Watercress
### *Rorippa nasturtium-aquaticum* (L.) Hayek

Watercress (also classified as *Nasturtium officinale* R. Br.) is an exotic plant of Eurasian origin. It grows in almost every state and in most of the Canadian provinces. The plants are easily identified, for they dwell in slow-moving water, blooming in late summer. The white flowers and the elongated fruit (siliques), shown in the illustration, are typical of the Brassicaceae as a whole. Watercress leaves are crisp with a peppery taste, more pronounced in wild than in cultivated plants. (Warning: the water in which the cress grows may be contaminated with the intestinal protozoan parasite *Giardia lamblia*.) The name *Rorippa* is said to be derived from the Anglo-Saxon word for the plant. The Latin species name *nasturtium-aquaticum* means "water nasturtium," from the similar peppery taste of watercress and the South American "nasturtium," a member of the genus *Tropaeolum*. Nasturtium, as used for the watercress, was derived, it is said, from Pliny's use of *nasium tormento* meaning "twisted nose," to describe the plant's piquancy.

## Weedy Imports

Many crucifers common in our mountains and elsewhere are not native plants, but are imported Eurasian weeds. They often grow in great numbers, usually on disturbed ground. Here are several of the most common of these weeds.

### Blue mustard (left)
### *Chorispora tenella* (Pall.) DC.

This common weed—it is sometimes known as the "cross-flower"—is easily identified, for there is no other crucifer in our area with similar small, four-petaled, light-purple flowers. It seems to be spreading rapidly in Idaho. The name *Chorispora,* derived from two Greek words, means "separate seed" for the configuration of the seeds in the plant's silique. If cows browse on this plant, their milk will have an unpleasant taste.

### Whitetop (above)
### *Cardaria draba* (L.) Desv.

The whitetop, (also heartpod hoary cress) has compact, flat-topped flower clusters that bloom from the outside in. It is further identified by its rather succulent serrated leaves and heart-shaped silicles. It blooms from early spring through the summer, sometimes forming immense patches on disturbed ground.

### Field pennycress (left)
### *Thlaspi arvense* L.

Field pennycress grows on disturbed dry ground. It is so common a weed that most will recognize it at first glance. Its common name, "pennycress," is derived from its disc-shaped silicles. A similar weed, the shepherd's purse, *Capsella bursa-pastoris* (L.) Medik., not shown here, takes its name from its triangular fruiting bodies.

### Spring whitlow-grass (above)
### *Draba verna* L.

As with the other weeds shown here, the spring whitlow-grass has spread throughout much of the Northern Hemisphere. It is easily identified by clustered bright-white flowers. The flowers are unusual for they have two pairs of opposed, deeply cleft petals—an identifying feature.

## Cactus Family (Cactaceae)

The Swedish botanist Carl Linnaeus (1707-1778) published his *Species Plantarum*, the basis for our modern system of binomial plant classification, in 1753. Challenged to find names for the many plants that he listed, he often used ones mentioned by ancient writers. He knew of American cacti, and he bestowed on them the Greek name *kaktos* believing that ours were related to a relative of the artichoke that the Greeks knew by that name. Later, the cacti were classified as a separate family, one that contains about 1,700 species. Cactaceae are New World plants (a cactus [*Rhipsalis* sp.] from Madagascar and southern Africa may have been introduced), ranging throughout the Americas from British Columbia to the southern ends of Chile and Argentina. The cacti have adapted superbly to the extremes of heat and dryness encountered in desert environments. In most, the leaves have been replaced with spines, and photosynthesis goes on in their fleshy stems. Some bear edible fruit. The stems take many forms: round, flattened, cylindrical, etc., and are often ribbed. The flowers are usually solitary, often showy, and have many sepals, petals, and stamens. Four species of cactus are found in Idaho, growing to montane elevations. The two shown on the opposite page are the ones most commonly encountered.

### Brittle cactus
### *Opuntia fragilis*
### (Nutt.) Haw.

The small ground-hugging brittle cactus grows as high as the montane zone, nestling against exposed rocks that hold the day's heat. At these higher elevations the plants—usually green—take on a reddish hue. The name, *fragilis*, reflects the ease with which segments break off the main stem and attach themselves to passers-by. Showy flowers last only a day or so, followed by spiny red fruit. The fragile cactus grows throughout the western part of the United States (excepting in Nevada and California) and Canada.

### Spiny prickly pear
### *Opuntia polyacantha* Haw.

The spiny cactus favors desert-like surroundings, growing to fairly high elevations. The flat stem joints are covered with many spines, the meaning of *polyacantha*. Attractive flowers range from a light yellow to bright red. *Opuntia polyacantha* is found throughout the western United States and Canada. One might guess that the name *opuntia* was derived from a Native American word, but no, it was that of a now unknown plant that grew near the city of Opus in ancient Greece.

**Nipple cactus**
*Escobaria missouriensis* (Sweet) D. R. Hunt var. *missouriensis*

The nipple cactus in Idaho is restricted to a few mountain valleys that drain into the Salmon River in Custer county. Often, only the flower-bearing portion extends above ground level so it is a plant that is easily missed. Its attractive, yellow-centered flowers are followed by small red fruit. Until fairly recently, the nipple cactus was classified as *Coryphantha missouriensis*, a name used in older guide books. An earlier name, *Mammilaria*, took note of the plants' "mammilate tubercles," the rounded and grooved, spine-bearing projections that explain the name, "nipple cactus." Several varieties are recognized, although this variety is the one found in Idaho. The species, in one or another of its varieties, ranges from the Rocky Mountain states across the Great Plains, east to Minnesota and Oklahoma, and west to Idaho and Arizona (apparently skipping Utah and Nevada). Its generic name, *Escobaria*, honors two Mexican brothers, Numa Pompilio Escobar Zerman (1874-1949) and Romulo Escobar Zerman (1882-1946). (See *California Plant Names*: *www.calflora.net/botanicalnames*.) "Missouri fox-tail cactus" has been proposed as a standard common name for the plant.

# Honeysuckle Family (Caprifoliaceae)

The Honeysuckle family includes five genera and about 210 species. Most are found in the Americas and in Eurasia where many are Mediterranean plants. Most are hardy shrubs and vines, including various honeysuckles and snowberries, commercially important as garden plants.

Although we will treat all of the plants shown here as Caprifoliaceae, it should be noted that five genera and approximately 245 species were recently assigned to the moschatel (Adoxaceae) family. Members of the latter family, including elderberries and viburnums, are mostly found in more temperate climates, as far north as the arctic regions of the Northern Hemisphere. Taken together, as was traditionally done until the 1990s, the members of these two families have flowers with five petals joined to form a basal tube, and five sepals. The leaves are mostly opposite and lack petioles (stemlets). Twinned flowers and fruit are common, as with the common garden honeysuckle.

Caprifoliaceae, the honeysuckle family's scientific name, was derived from an old word "caprifoil" used for the European honeysuckle *Lonicera periclymenum*. Caprifoil, in turn, came from the Latin *caprifolium*, a word derived from the Latin *caper* for "goat" and *folium* for "leaf." There is some suggestion that the name for the plant may have originated on the island of Capri, where goats were common.

Finally, twinflower (*Linnaea borealis* L., not shown), a creeping evergreen subshrub that grows in our northern mountains, was long included in the honeysuckle family; it is now assigned to its own family, Linnaeaceae.

**Trumpet honeysuckle**
*Lonicera ciliosa*
**(Pursh) Poir. ex DC.**

The attractive, orange-flowered trumpet honeysuckle vine is often seen growing along roadsides and trails to montane elevations. It is native to the four northwestern states, British Columbia, and to the northern part of California. It is easily identified by its clustered, bright orange, trumpet-shaped flowers and by a pair of joined opposing leaves just below the flower cluster through which the stem passes. The plant was unknown to science until Lewis and Clark returned to the United States with a dried specimen that they had collected on June 5, 1806, while camped on the Clearwater River near today's Kamiah, Idaho close to where this plant was photographed.

### Utah honeysuckle
### *Lonicera utahensis* S. Watson

The Utah honeysuckle grows in the mountains of Idaho from mid-elevation nearly to treeline. Its small flowers are neatly paired and their ovaries mature into two red berries that sometimes fuse into hourglass-shaped fruit. An attractive shrub, it is often used in ornamental landscaping. Lewis and Clark collected a specimen of the Utah honeysuckle, most likely while ascending the North Fork of the Salmon River, on September 2, 1805.

### Twinberry
### *Lonicera involucrata* (Richardson) Banks ex Spreng.

The twinberry is a shrub found along water courses as high as the subalpine zone. Inconspicuous twinned yellow flowers appear in the spring and by mid-summer paired, inedible, blue-black berries appear. These form above two red leaves, or "bracts." Together these are known as an "involucre" from which the plant derives its species name. The bracts are commonly a subdued deep red, but under favorable conditions turn a bright waxy scarlet as in our illustration. The genus *Lonicera*—which takes its name from Adam Lonitzer (1528-1586), a German botanist—consists of about 180 species. Meriwether Lewis collected this plant near today's misnamed Lewis and Clark Pass* on the continental divide in Montana during the expedition's return journey (July 7, 1806). Although Lewis did not know it at the time, the plant had previously been described. Today it is occasionally used as an ornamental garden plant.

---

* "misnamed" because only Lewis crossed the pass. William Clark was far to the south, heading for the three forks of the Missouri River and from there to the Yellowstone River.

**Common snowberry**
***Symphoricarpos albus*** (L.) S. F. Blake

The common snowberry is found throughout our western mountains and in all of the northern states and Canadian provinces, growing at mid-elevations. It is commonly encountered along our trails and roadsides. Our plant is var. *laevigatus* S. F. Blake; the varietal name means "smooth." It was unknown to science until collected by the Lewis and Clark expedition, probably somewhere along the Missouri River on an unknown date. This snowberry been used as an ornamental shrub almost from the time the explorers' specimen (dried fruit) grew out from their seeds, planted in Philadelphia. It remains a popular garden plant today. The mushy white berries, shown below, have no food value.

**Mountain snowberry**
***Symphoricarpos oreophilus*** A. Gray

The mountain snowberry replaces the common snowberry at higher altitudes. It is found all along our hiking trails, and is easily recognized by its distinctive soft blue-green oval leaves. In late spring, the shrubs bear the small white tubular flowers shown above. They are usually borne in pairs, with petals that flare out a bit at the end. The generic name *Symphoricarpos* is derived from three Greek words that mean "fruit that is born together" in pairs. The species name *oreophilus* also is from the Greek and means "mountain lover." This plant's berries, shown below, are smaller and oval-shaped compared to those of the common snowberry.

**Western blue elder (left)**
*Sambucus cerulea* Raf.

**Western black elder (right)**
*Sambucus racemosa* L.
var. *melanocarpa* (A. Gray) McMinn

The two elders shown here grow as shrubs or small trees. The plants are quite similar. Both are native to most of our western states and Canadian provinces. Elders are often seen growing along stream banks and in permanently moist areas as high as the subalpine zone. Their compound leaves are odd pinnate, each has seven toothed leaflets. As the illustrations suggest, the flower clusters of the two species differ slightly. The blue elder's flower cluster is flat-topped, whereas the black elder has cone-shaped clusters. The color of their fruit is reflected in their names; the species name *cerulea* means blue and the varietal name of the western black elder *melanocarpa*, means "black fruit." The name, *Sambucus*, is derived from the Latin name for an Old World elder; the species name *racemosa* was derived from "raceme," a botanical term for a flower cluster that blooms from the bottom upward. Elderberries ripen in late summer and are often used to make jellies and wine. The berries do not last long in the wild, for they are a favorite of birds and animals.

# Pink Family (Caryophyllaceae)

The pink family is moderately large, consisting of 93 genera and 2,400 species scattered throughout the north temperate zone; many are found in northern Mediterranean countries. The family is also well represented in our Northwest. While many of the European species are colorful, ours are mostly rather unprepossessing, small, white flowers. Typically, plants in the pink family have narrow, opposed leaves that originate from swollen nodes along the stem. The flowers are usually five-petaled and the ends of the petals are often notched or fringed. In some species the sepals coalesce to form a swollen tube. Ornamental plants and cut flowers, especially species of *Dianthus* (carnations, sweet william, for example), have considerable economic importance. A few of our Caryophyllaceae are weeds, including several garden ornamentals imported from Europe that now grow wild in the western United States. These include bouncingbet (*Saponaria officianalis*), babysbreath (*Gypsophila paniculata*), chickweed (*Stellaria media*) and several others.

The scientific name Caryophyllaceae is derived from the Greek word for the clove pink, a relative of the carnation that smells like cloves; in fact, the Greek word for cloves and for the plant are the same, *garyphallo*. This word, in turn, evolved from the Greek words *karyon* for "nut" and *phyllon* for "leaf," combined to describe a clove—a dried bud of the clove tree (*Syzygium aromaticum*).

## Uinta sandwort,
### *Eremogone kingii* (S. Watson) Ikonn. var. *glabrescens* (S. Watson) Dorn

The Uinta sandwort is a low, spreading plant that grows at all elevations on rocky sagebrush covered slopes and gravelly ridges, blooming from late spring well into the summer. Brown anthers borne on thin filaments overlie each petal and give the five-petaled flowers a spotted appearance. Until recently, this and similar plants were included in genus *Arenaria*, a term derived from the Latin word *arena* meaning "sand" reflecting the plants' preferred habitat. Other sandworts found in Idaho are quite similar in appearance; identification, at least at the generic level, should not be a problem. This plant's species name honors geologist Clarence King (1842-1901) who surveyed the Rocky Mountains and Great Basin, in the 1860s. *Eremogone*, from two Greek words, means "solitary seed."

## Field chickweed
### *Cerastium arvense* L.

The field chickweed is a common, widely distributed wildflower that grows at all elevations. It is found in much of North America as well as in Eurasia. It is characterized by deeply notched petals and narrow, opposing, gray-green leaves. The name *Cerastium* was derived from a Greek word, *kerastos*—meaning "horn"—for the shape of its seed capsules. The species name, *arvense*, from the Latin, implies an open meadow, reflecting the plant's growth preference. Cerastium cultivars are often used as ornamental border plants.

## Sticky chickweed,
### *Pseudostellaria jamesiana* (Torr.) W. A. Weber & R. L. Hartm.

The sticky chickweed is a pretty little five-petaled late May-blooming flower that prefers shaded places. The plant is found in all of our western states including Texas. It may be identified by its ridged leaves and dainty notched petals. Edwin James (1797-1861), for whom the species was named, was a surgeon-naturalist with the Long Expedition that explored Colorado's Rocky Mountains in 1820. The name chickweed comes from related European species that apparently are a favorite food of poultry. The common name "sticky starwort" has been suggested for this plant to avoid confusion with other chickweeds.

## Menzies silene
### *Silene menziesii* Hook.

Menzies silene has clustered small flowers each having five lobed white petals. The petals have two inner tab-like appendages at their base, a common feature of flowers of this genus, although not always easily seen. Silenes also have enlarged calyx tubes, although they are not as prominent in this species as in others. This small plant favors open woods, growing to fairly high elevations. It is found throughout the West, south to Arizona and New Mexico, and north to Alaska. Its name honors Archibald Menzies, surgeon-naturalist with the Vancouver Expedition. He collected many new-to-science plants during the exploration of our Northwest.

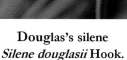

### Douglas's silene
### *Silene douglasii* Hook.

Douglas's silene is found in the Rocky Mountains, and west to the Pacific coast, growing from plains to high in the mountains. It is characterized by opposing linear stem leaves and notched petals. Its calyx tube is smoother and less hairy than those of related plants. The species name refers to plant-hunter David Douglas whom we have met often on these pages.

As a group, silenes tend to be "glandular"; many small surface glands secrete sticky fluid, some are sticky enough to capture insects, hence the common name "catchfly," long used for plants in this and related genera. The shape of the prominent calyx tubes helps to identify the species.

### Parry's silene
### *Silene parryi* (S. Watson)
### C. L. Hitchc. & Maguire

Parry's silene blooms from early summer on, according to the altitude; it ranges as high as treeline. It is a long stemmed, plant with a cluster of basal lanceolate leaves. It may be further identified by small, notched petals that barely protrude from the end of its square-based, bottle-shaped calyx tube formed by five joined and pointed sepals. As the flowers age, ten longitudinal green stripes on the calyces turn deep purple. The plant is found from British Columbia and Alberta, throughout the Northwest, and south to Idaho, Oregon and Wyoming. Charles Christopher Parry (1823-1890), for whom this species is named, was an English-born American botanist. Several other western plants bear his name.

### Scouler's silene
### *Silene scouleri* Hook.

Scouler's silene is found in most of the western mountain states and Canadian provinces. At least three, and usually more, pairs of broadly lanceolate, opposing leaves become increasingly smaller and farther apart as they ascend the stem. Higher up there are two or more clusters of long tubed flowers with hairy, sticky calyces. Scouler's silene is a rather common species, found mostly at lower altitudes. The variety shown here is var. *concolor* (Greene) C. L. Hitchc. & Maguire.

This plant's species name honors John Scouler (1804-1871), a ship's surgeon who came to America in 1825 with David Douglas. Douglas remained, and Scouler returned with his ship to England, having found several new plants during his brief stay in the Northwest.

# Goosefoot Family (Chenopodiaceae)

The goosefoot family is moderately large, made up of 97 genera and 1,300 species world-wide, and it is well represented in the United States. Both the common and scientific names were derived from the goosefoot plant, *Chenopodium album* (*chenopodium*, from the Greek, means "goose's foot"), formerly used in Europe as a potherb known as "lambs-quarters" and "fat-hen." (The plant also occurs throughout North America where it is known as the common pigweed.)

The family is chiefly notable for those species that are important as food plants. These include spinach (*Spinacea oleracea*) which has largely displaced lambs-quarters as a green; Swiss chard and beets (*Beta vulgaris* subsp. *vulgaris*) whose cultivars include both edible beets and sugar beets; blites (formerly included in the genus *Blitum*, now classified as species of *Chenopodium*), illustrated on the next page; and the South American cereal, quinoa (*Chenopodium quinoa*).

Some of the Chenopodiaceae are troublesome weeds, including various xerophytic and salt-loving (halophytic) species. Weedy chenopods seem to spring up over night on newly disturbed ground. Many members of the family, including spinach, contain oxalic acid, a substance that can be poisonous if ingested in large amounts; it may also contribute to the formation of oxalate contaning kidney stones.

### Strawberry blite
### *Chenopodium capitatum* (L.) Ambrosi

One may be surprised and curious on first seeing this chenopod, for the fruit looks for all the world like a ripe raspberry. We have included it here because the plant is not well known, and anyone who hikes in our mountains will sooner or later encounter the strawberry blite—a plant notable for its fruit, rather than for its small and unimpressive flowers (not shown).

The strawberry blite is an edible native plant that grows to higher elevations in our mountains. It is widely distributed, found in all but the southern Great Plains states and those of the deep south. It also grows in northern Asia and Europe. It was, in fact, described by Linnaeus (indicated by the "L." following the scientific name). Its species name, *capitatum,* means "growing in a head," although why that was used for this plant is uncertain. The word "blite" (sometimes written, incorrectly, as "blight") is a term that goes back to ancient Greece (*bliton*) where it may have been used for this plant, and for other edible chenopods. Despite their succulent appearance, its wild strawberry-like berries are tasteless.

## Cleome Family (Cleomaceae)

The cleome family is small, consisting of 11 genera and about 300 species. Most members grow in the temperate zones of both the Old and the New World; a few are found in Idaho, including the two plants shown on the following page. The cleome family is closely related to both the mustard family (Brassicaceae) and the caper family (Capparaceae). The relationship of the three families is so close, in fact, that some botanists include all three in the mustard family. The family has little economic importance other than the use of several members—the cleomes especially—as ornamental garden plants.

### Rocky Mountain beeplant
#### *Cleome serrulata* Pursh

Despite its common name, the Rocky Mountain beeplant is not restricted to the Rocky Mountains. Originally found only in the West and Midwest, it now grows in the Northeast as an introduced plant. In Idaho, it is found growing as high as montane foothills. Beeplants are easily identified by their tall stems surrounded by short, narrow, three-lobed leaves. Thanks to their clustered, attractive, four-petaled, long-anthered flowers they are often grown as ornamentals. Bees are attracted to their flowers, further adding to their appeal. Lewis and Clark collected the Rocky Mountain beeplant in South Dakota in August of 1804; the plant was then new to science.

### Yellow beeplant
#### *Cleome lutea* Hook.

A closely related plant, the yellow beeplant has remained west of the Mississippi, growing most commonly near standing water. We are including it here, for it is said to occur in Idaho's mountains as a montane plant, although—unlike the Rocky Mountain beeplant—we have not seen it growing that high. Cleomes were used by Native Americans for their edible seeds and the young plants were used as potherbs. Thorough boiling is necessary before the plants can be eaten, for the plants have a most unpleasant odor.

## Dogwood Family
## Cornaceae

The dogwood family is a small one, made up of one genus and 60 species. It is represented in our Northwest by three species. Two of these are flowering trees, and one is a small non-woody plant. All are attractive, well suited for use in gardens and ornamental landscaping—the family's chief economic importance. Their blooms are characterized by large, petal-like white bracts, usually four, but sometimes as many as seven, and by centrally clustered small and inconspicuous flowers.

The origin of the generic name *Cornus*—from which both the family name Cornaceae, and the alternate common name, "cornel" (used more often in Europe), were derived—is in doubt. The word means "horn" in Latin; possibly referring to the trees' hard wood. The origin of "dogwood" is said to have been from skewers ("dogs") that butchers in the distant past made from the hard wood of the European dogwood, *Cornus sanguinea*.* The *Oxford English Dictionary* lists "dogwood" as being used first in 1676, in a citation describing "a fine Flower-bearing-Tree" that grew in Virginia, referring to the flowering dogwood, *Cornus florida*.

---

* I have been unable to find documented use of the word "dog" to mean a skewer *per se*. Nevertheless, the OED (*q.v.*) gives several examples of "dogs" used as sharp tools to fix or fasten objects.

### Bunchberry
### *Cornus canadensis* L.

The bunchberry is a ground-dwelling, non-woody plant, widely distributed across northern North America, west to Asia, and east to Greenland. It is found in all of our northwestern and northern tier states as far south as Colorado and (rarely) in New Mexico, growing in shaded, moist forest surroundings. The plants have a rosette of five or six deep green leaves. In early summer four large white bracts, and later, bright red berries make the plants immediately identifiable. In common with other dogwoods, the bunchberry's actual flowers are tiny. Bunchberries do well in ornamental gardens.

Meriwether Lewis might have seen bunchberries fruiting during the expedition's east-to-west September crossing of the Bitterroot and Clearwater ranges in 1805. We know that he saw the plants flowering in Idaho during the spring of the following year, for he collected a specimen on June 16, 1806, as the expedition made its first attempt to ascend the Lolo Trail.

### Red-osier dogwood
### *Cornus sericea* L. (above and right))

The red-osier dogwood is a red-barked shrub or small tree that grows throughout Canada and in all but our southern states. The ovaries of its clustered small, four-petaled flowers mature into white berries. "Osier," Latin for "willow," is a word used for any pliant branches that are suitable for basket-making. the Latin species name *sericea* means "silky," for the fine hair on the the leaves. Lewis and Clark wrote in the winter of 1804-1805, while at Fort Mandan, that Indians smoked the bark of the red-osier dogwood mixed with tobacco, to stretch the tobacco supply. Both plants on this page are favored by landscape gardeners.

### Western flowering-dogwood (right)
### *Cornus nuttallii* Audubon

The western dogwood grows mostly west of the Cascade range, but a few trees are also found along Idaho's Clearwater River. Its resemblance to the eastern flowering dogwood, *Cornus florida* L., may explain why Meriwether Lewis did not collect it in the spring of 1806. Later, Thomas Nuttall recognized that it was a new species. John James Audubon (1785-1851) included the western flowering dogwood in one of his illustrations by way of thanking Nuttall for the use of ornithological material. This was the first published description of the tree, so Audubon is credited with establishing the scientific name.

Band-tailed Dove or Pigeon.
1. Male. 2. Female.
Cornus nuttalli

**NUTTALL'S DOG-WOOD**

CORNUS NUTTALLII *Audubon*

This very beautiful tree, which was discovered by Mr. **NUTTALL** on the Columbia river, attains a height of fifty feet or more, and is characterized by its smooth reddish-brown bark; large, ovate, acuminate leaves, and conspicuous flowers, with six obovate, acute, involucral bracteas, which are rose-coloured at the base, white towards the end, veined and reticulated with light purple. The berries are oblong, and of a bright carmine.*

The Band-Tailed Dove or Pigeon
*Columba fasciata* Say

Image and the first published description of *Cornus nuttallii* from:
*The Birds of America from Drawings Made in the United States and Their Territories*
*by John James Audubon F.R.SS. L.E.E.*
New York, 1842, Vol. IV, page 312

---

*Although Audubon described six "involucral bracteas," the number varies from four to seven.

## Stonecrop Family (Crassulaceae)

The stonecrop family consists of 33 genera and approximately 1,500 species. Crassulaceae are found on all continents with the exception of Australia and Antarctica. Most of its members are thick-leaved succulents. The family takes its scientific name from the word *crassula*, an older generic term for the sedums and now a name of another genus in the family. The word probably was derived from the Latin *crassus*, meaning "thick," for the succulent leaves found throughout the family. The only economic importance of the Crassulaceae is that many—for example, the jade plant (*Crassula ovata*) from East Africa, the flowering red kalanchoe (*Kalanchoe blossfeldiana*) from Madagascar, and hen and chickens plants (*Jovibarba* spp.)–are popular ornamentals. *Sedum* is the largest genus in the family.

**Wormleaf stonecrop, *Sedum stenopetalum* Pursh (left)**

**Lanceleaf stonecrop, *Sedum lanceolatum* Torr. (center & below)**

The two stonecrops shown here are closely related plants with similar yellow flowers and the thick leaves typical of sedums in general. They each have distinguishing characteristics. The leaves of the wormleaf stonecrop tend to stand away from the stem, whereas those of the lanceleaf stonecrop remain appressed. Similarly, when the follicles (dried seed capsules) of the plants are ripe, the wormleaf stonecrop's follicles protrude horizontally, whereas those of the lanceleaf plant are borne nearly upright. Finally, the wormleaf sedum retain its leaves when the plant is in full flower, whereas those of the lanceleaf sedum are shed (as shown in the illustration below). Thanks to water stored in the leaves, stonecrops thrive when rooted in the organic debris that collects in rocky cracks and depressions, without need of soil water—a phenomenon that explains the common name, "stonecrop." Both plants grow from low to high elevations, almost always on rocks, or on rocky soil; we have seen lanceleaf sedum quite at home on alpine tundra. The lanceleaf plant grows as far south as Arizona and New Mexico, north to Alaska and east to the Great Plains. The wormleaf stonecrop is a native of the northwestern states, and the two adjacent Canadian provinces.

Meriwether Lewis collected both plants, on the same day (July 1, 1806) while camped at Traveler's Rest near today's Missoula, Montana; both are on the same specimen sheet in the Lewis and Clark Herbarium at the Academy of Natural Sciences in Philadelphia.

# Heath Family (Ericaceae)

Ericaceae, the scientific name for the heath family, was derived from a Greek name for a now unknown heath. The family is made up of 140 genera and approximately 3,000 species of shrubs and trees. Most prefer acidic soil and the cooler temperatures of temperate zones, growing often in moist shaded areas, along streams and on mountain slopes. Although the leaves are usually opposite, they may be alternate or whorled. The flowers have four or five sepals and four to seven petals. The petals are often joined at the base to form a tube so that the flowers are urn- or bell-shaped. Many members of the family are commercially important for their fruit (*Vaccinium* spp.: blueberries, cranberries and related shrubs; and *Gaylusacia* spp.: the huckleberries*); others are important as decorative garden plants including species of *Rhododendron* (a genus that also includes Labrador tea and azaleas). Four members of the heath family are state flowers: *Rhododendron maximum* for West Virginia, and *Rhododendron californicum* for Washington. The mountain laurel *(Kalmia latifolia)* is Pennsylvania's state flower, and the fragrant and secretive mayflower or trailing arbutus (*Epigaea repens*) is the state flower of Massachusetts.

*There is considerable local variation in the use of common names for the berries in these two genera, and many names are used: blueberries, huckleberries, bilberries, whortleberries, etc. Recent tendency is to place the huckleberries in *Gaylussacia*, the blueberries remain in *Vaccinium*.

### Trapper's tea (left, below left)
### *Rhododendron neoglandulosum* Harmaja

Trapper's tea (formerly *Ledum glandulosum*) is a western subapine to alpine plant that blooms in early summer. Its large white flowerheads, set off by deep green leaves, are striking. The fruit is a small brownish capsule that contains numerous seeds. The derivation of the name, "trapper's tea" is uncertain, but presumably the leaves were used for tea in the distant past. Readers should not emulate our pioneer forebears, because the plant is poisonous.

### Rusty menziesia, *Menziesia ferruginea* Sm. (below)

Rusty menziesia (also "false azalea" and "fool's huckleberry") honors Archibald Menzies who first collected the plant. It is an attractive deciduous shrub that grows from California to Alaska, and inland to the northern Rocky Mountains. The plants prefer moist surroundings, and are often found in the company of trapper's tea. Urn-shaped flowers, ranging in color from rust to bright red, help to identify the plant. The fruit is inedible, hence the common name "fool's huckleberry." Menziesias are sometimes used as ornamental shrubs in moist situations.

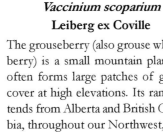

**Grouseberry (left and below left)**
*Vaccinium scoparium*
**Leiberg ex Coville**

The grouseberry (also grouse whortleberry) is a small mountain plant that often forms large patches of ground cover at high elevations. Its range extends from Alberta and British Columbia, throughout our Northwest, south to California and New Mexico, and east to Montana and South Dakota. The plants have many thin branches and if bundled would form a serviceable broom (*scoparium* means broom-like). In good years the plants bear many little flowers typical of those of other *Vaccinium* species (blueberries, cranberries, etc.). These ripen into the red berries shown here. They are sweet and taste like blueberries. Other vacciniums grow in our mountains, but the grouseberry is the most common subalpine species.

**Kinnikinnick (above, above left)**
*Arctostaphylos uva-ursi*
**(L.) Spreng.**

Kinnikinnick (also bearberry) is a circumboreal plant found throughout the northern United States and Canada, north to Alaska and south to Arizona and Virginia. It is a ground-hugging plant that forms tight mats. Oval leathery leaves and urn-shaped early-blooming white flowers mature into bright red berries. The fruit is not really palatable, but Native Americans apparently used it as a component of pemmican. A fur trader gave Lewis and Clark a specimen of kinnikinnick while they were overwintering at the Mandan Villages in today's North Dakota (1804-1805). He told them that the Indians mixed leaves of kinnikinnick with the bark of the red-osier dogwood (page 93) and with tobacco to stretch the tobacco supply. Kinnikinnick grows in our mountains mostly from the Salmon River northward, in moist or shady locations, although we have also seen it growing on alpine tundra further south.

### Merten's mountain heather
### *Cassiope mertensiana* (Bong.) G. Don
### *var. gracilis* (Piper) C. L. Hitchc.

The three mountain plants shown here are subalpine and alpine plants that grow in high wet meadows and on the banks of mountain lakes, often in each other's company. This mountain heather and the pink mountain heather shown below are so closely related that they often hybridize when growing close to each other. Both plants are native to western coastal and Rocky Mountains states (although this variety is found only in Oregon, Idaho and Montana). The name *Cassiope* is from Greek mythology, the name of Andromeda's mother. The species name honors German botanist Franz Karl Merten whom we have met before.

### Pink mountain heather
### *Phyllodoce empetriformis* (Sm.) D. Don.

Both this and the mountain heather shown above are low evergreen plants. This one's flowers are pink rather than white and its joined petals roll outward along their margins. Phyllodoce was a water nymph in Greek mythology. Why the names of mythological Greek characters were applied to alpine heathers is a mystery; *empetriformis,* from the Greek, means "on rocks." Frederick Pursh in his 1813 *Flora* reported seeing a Lewis and Clark specimen that was probably gathered in north-central Idaho (the present location of the specimen is unknown). Attempts to cultivate this lovely little alpine plant have ended in failure.

### Alpine laurel
### *Kalmia microphylla* (Hook.) A. Heller

Our alpine laurel is closely related to the state flower of Pennsylvania, *Kalmia latifolia*, a white-flowered shrub or small tree often used in ornamental landscaping. Our plant is only a few inches tall—an adaptation to its alpine surroundings. The relationship between the two plants is confirmed by this plant's woody stem and almost identically shaped flowers. As with the two mountain heathers shown above, the alpine laurel prefers wet mountain meadows and bogs, where it blooms soon after snowmelt. Its distribution is similar to that of the other two plants. Alpine laurel is poisonous to cattle and sheep—not usually a problem, given the altitude at which it grows.

### Pink wintergreen (left)
### *Pyrola asarifolia* Michx.

This generic name *Pyrola* was derived from a Latin *pyrus,* for "pear" because of similar shaped leaves in some species of wintergreen. The name *asarifolia* suggests that the leaves resemble those of the wild ginger (*Asarum caudatum*). The pink wintergreen is a reclusive plant, often found at higher elevations. Nodding pink flowers form a loose cluster atop a bare stem. Each has five dainty pink petals, ten stamens and a single protruding style.

### Green wintergreen (right)
### *Pyrola chlorantha* Sw.

As both common and scientific names suggest, the green wintergreen has light green-petaled flowers (*chlorantha*, from the Greek, means "green flower"). It grows in partial shade, often in conifer forests. In common with the other wintergreens, it blooms in mid-summer.

### White-vein wintergreen (left)
### *Pyrola picta* Sm.

While this plant's flowers are similar to those of our other pyrolas, its patterned basal leaves make it stand out in the shaded forests where it grows. Most of the plants in the wintergreen family grow all across North America, but this plant is found only in the West and in the Black Hills of South Dakota.

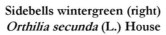

### Sidebells wintergreen (right)
### *Orthilia secunda* (L.) House

This little plant, while similar to the pyrolas, has somewhat different flowers. It is easily identified because its greenish white flowers grow on only one side of the stem (*secunda,* from the Latin, means "turned," or, in this context, "one sided"). It is a common plant and will be found blooming in mid- to late summer. As the name "wintergreen" implies, all of these plants are evergreen.

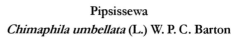

### Pipsissewa
### *Chimaphila umbellata* (L.) W. P. C. Barton

The pipsissewa, or prince's pine, is a shade-loving, evergreen plant that bears attractive parasol-shaped, five-petaled pink flowers. As with our other wintergreens, it grows in cool forest surroundings. The plant is found throughout the west, in the north-eastern states, in the Canadian provinces and in Eurasia. The species name *Chimaphila*, means "winter-lover" derived from its evergreen properties. This and other wintergreens have long been used medicinally both topically and in beverages, probably without any real therapeutic benefit.

A related plant, the little prince's pine (*Chimaphila menziesii* (R. Br. ex D. Don) Spreng., not shown) occurs in the mountains of central and northern Idaho. It has few flowers and its leaves are broadest near the base of the blade.

### One-flower Wintergreen
### *Moneses uniflora* (L.) A. Gray

The one-flower wintergreen (also single-delight, wood nymph, shy-maiden, and wax-flower) is a widely distributed plant that grows in all of our northern states, in the Rocky Mountain states, throughout Canada, and Eurasia. It grows in moist places as high as the subalpine zone. With its single (*uniflora*), five petaled, nodding white flower and rosette of basal leaves it is easy to identify. It is the only species in its genus. The name *Moneses* was derived from two Greek words, *monos* and *hesis*, meaning "single delight."

### Indian pipe
### *Monotropa uniflora* L.

The Indian pipe occurs in Idaho, although it is seen less commonly than the pinesap shown below. It is native to our northwestern states, Alaska, across Canada and in all of the eastern states. The two plants shown on this page are both saprophytes that thrive on forest litter. Plants in this genus lack chlorophyll and their root systems are always associated with minute fungi. The generic name *Monotropa* was derived from the Greek words, *mono* for "one" and *tropos* for "direction," evidently referring to plants that bear their flowers on one side of the stem.

### Pinesap
### *Monotropa hypopithys* L.

The pinesap is also found in most of the United States and in Eurasia. It is easily distinguished from the Indian pipe by its yellow color, turning brown as it matures. Several small flowers are clustered at the top of the stem, compared to the Indian pipe's single flower. The species name *hypopithys* was also derived from two Greek words, *hypo* for "under" and *pithys* for "pine," alluding to the pine forests in which the plants are usually found. Identification is usually not be a problem, although this plant and species of *Corallorhiza* in the orchid family are rather similar in appearance, and both are saprophytes that grow on shaded leaf-litter.

## Pea Family (Fabaceae)

The older scientific name for the pea family, Leguminosae, is one of several family names that don't end in "-aceae", so many botanists prefer Fabaceae (from the Latin word "faba," for "bean"). Either name is correct. The family is a large one and taxonomically difficult even for botanists. It is made up of more than 630 genera and approximately 18,000 species including herbs, vines, shrubs and trees. The pea family is second only to the grasses (Poaceae) in economic importance. The flowers of many of the family's plants are made up of five petals; these include a large upper petal, or "banner," two smaller lateral ones ("wings"), and the two lowest ones joined together to form a "keel." The flowers are commonly referred to as being "papilionaceous," a word derived from *papilion*, the Latin word for "butterfly." The fruit is commonly a pod that splits open along two seams. Leaves are compound: either pinnate (like a feather) or palmate (leaflets all arise from a central point like fingers from the palm). The family includes beans, peas, lentils, peanuts, clover, alfalfa, etc., plants important not only for their food value to man and domestic animals, but also for their ability to fix soil nitrogen. About twenty-five genera, including both native and introduced species, grow in the Northwest; many are found in our mountains. Although some have edible fruit, others are poisonous, so it is best to regard all wild leguminaceous plants as inedible.

---

### *Astragalus,* Milk-vetches

*Astragalus,* is a large genus with approximately 1,750 species worldwide. Well over one hundred species grow in our Northwest, and many are found in our mountains—only a few representative species can be shown here. The genus is characterized by pea-like, odd-pinnate leaves ("odd-pinnate" implies opposing leaflets in a feather like arrangement with a single leaflet at the end), and papilionaceous flowers. The plants typically are low with colorful white, yellow, or pink-to-purple flowers. They are often difficult to identify. The derivation of *astragalus* is interesting. Dried seed-containing pods of some species rattle when shaken, suggesting the sound of dice in a cup. In ancient times dice were made from the ankle bones of animals (sheep and goats especially). These were called "astragals," a word derived from the Greek word *astragalos* for ankle, hence *astragalus* for the plant.

---

### Pursh's milk-vetch
### *Astragalus purshii* Douglas ex Hook. var. *concinnus* Barneby

The milk-vetch shown on the left, *Astragalus purshii,* grows as high as the montane zone. There are many varietal forms. All have a prominent calyx and their flowers range in color from white through yellow to a purple-tinged pink, as in this illustration. The species name honors Frederick Pursh (1774-1820), the botanist who identified and published descriptions of many of the plants that Lewis and Clark collected. David Douglas first gathered this species and suggested that it be named to honor Pursh. The variety shown here is native to central Idaho and western Montana; the name *concinnus* means "neat" or "elegant."

### Canadian milk-vetch
### *Astragalus canadensis* L. var. *mortonii* (Nutt.) S. Watson

The Canadian milk-vetch is a common plant that grows from sea level to at least as high as the montane zone in our mountains. The species is found throughout North America, although the varietal form shown here grows only in the northwestern states and British Columbia. The plants spread by rhizomes to form distinctly circumscribed patches. They may also be identified by their unusually tall (for a milk-vetch) upright stems, congested clusters of yellowish-white pea-like flowers and, in our variety, by a calyx covered with black and white hairs. The variety, *mortonii,* was gathered by Nathaniel Wyeth in 1833 and named to honor Philadelphia naturalist Samuel George Morton (1799-1851).

### Indian milk-vetch (left)
### *Astragalus australis* (L.) Lam.
### var. *glabriusculus* (Hook.) Isley

Indian milk-vetch (formerly *Astragalus aboriginorum*) grows to treeline and above, on exposed, wind-swept, rocky soil. It is found throughout the northern Rocky Mountains, and neighboring states, in the two western Canadian provinces, and in Alaska as well as in Europe and in eastern Russia. The plants vary from place to place, but typically the banner is erect, the flowers are whitish and often have purple markings on the keel and the ends of the wings are slightly notched. The leaves have seven to fifteen closely ranked leaflets. Its roots are said to be edible.

### Bent-flowered milk-vetch (left)
### *Astragalus vexilliflexus* Sheldon
### var. *nubilus* Barneby

The bent-flowered milk-vetch is a tiny-leaved, small-flowered, densely matted plant that stands only an inch or so high. Although the species *vexilliflexus* is found in the Rocky Mountains of Alberta to Wyoming, the varietal form, *nubilus* shown here, occurs only in central Idaho's Custer County. (The plant was photographed well above treeline on Mt. Borah in the Lost River Range.) The species name, *vexilliflexus*, means, roughly "flexed standard," referring to the banner. The varietal name, *nubilus*, means grayish-blue, for the leaves.

### Northern yellow crazyweed
### *Oxytropis campestris* (L.) DC
### var. *cusickii* (Greenm.) Barneby

The northern yellow crazyweed is a variable, far flung species. Twelve varieties are recognized; var. *cusickii* is the only one found in Idaho. The plant grows as high as the alpine zone, where this plant was photographed. It is a low plant at this altitude, with odd-pinnate leaves, each with seventeen, or fewer, leaflets. The species, in its many varieties, grows all across Canada and western United States, south to Utah and Colorado, west to Oregon and Washington, and east to Minnesota. It is also native to Eurasia.

### Bessey's crazyweed
### *Oxytropis besseyi* (Rydb.) Blank. var. *salmonensis* Barneby

Bessey's crazyweed grows in Alberta, Idaho, Montana, Wyoming, Nevada, Utah and, uncommonly, in Colorado and Saskatchewan. The plant is characterized by gray-green, furry leaves, and longish stems topped with tight clusters of brightly colored red, or reddish-purple flowers. All parts of the plant save the flower petals, are noticeably hairy. Half a dozen varieties of Bessey's crazyweed are recognized, differentiated by differences in size, distribution and type of hairs, etc. The species as a whole is relatively common, although the variety shown here is not, for it is found only in Idaho where it grows in dry mountain valleys that drain into the Salmon River south of Challis. The plant favors rocky ground, blooming at the same time as the nearby desert phlox (*Phlox austromontana* Coville).

### Late yellow crazyweed
### *Oxytropis monticola* A. Gray

The crazyweeds (also known as "locoweeds") take their common name from the poisonous effect they have on grazing animals. The scientific name, *Oxytropis*, means "sharp-keel" for a pointed leading edge where two lower petals are fused. Typically, short-stemmed, papilionaceous flowers are borne on an erect stem. The leaves are made up of varying numbers of leaflets with a single terminal leaflet; they are "odd-pinnate." A subalpine and alpine plant, it occurs in Washington, eastern Oregon, central Idaho, and east to Alberta, the Dakotas and Colorado. The species name, *monticola*, means "mountain-loving." The plant, also known as the mountain crazyweed, was formerly classified as *Oxytropis campestris* var. *gracilis*.

### Nevada pea
### *Lathyrus lanszwertii* Kellogg var. *aridus* (Piper) Jepson

*Lathyrus*, a name used by ancient Greeks for the European chickpea. Plants in this genus are commonly known as "vetchlings," or "sweet peas"; the latter from the related and long cultivated European sweet pea, *Lathyrus odoratus* L. They are rambling, climbing plants whose compound leaves typically have the one or more tendrils at the end of the feather-like compound leaves (some species lack tendrils).

The Nevada pea (also "Lanszwert's vetchling" or "thick-leaved pea") is often seen growing in high foothills to montane ponderosa pine forests, distinguished by its large, white, or purple- or pink-tinged (var. *lanszwertii*), papilionaceous flowers borne in small clusters. The plants are found in most western states, from the Pacific coast, east to Idaho and south to Texas. The species is named for a Belgian-born California pharmacist, Louis Lanszweert (1825-1888).

**Mountain thermopsis**
***Thermopsis rhombifolia* Nutt.**
**var. *montana* (Nutt. ex Torr. & A. Gray) Isley**

The mountain thermopsis (or mountain golden pea) is a tall, showy plant that would be quite at home in an ornamental garden (the plants, in fact, do well when grown from seeds). Bright yellow, loosely clustered flowers and clover-like leaves help to identify it. The name *Thermopsis* comes from two Greek words: the first was used for lupines, and *-opsis* is an an ending that means "looks like." Two varieties of this plant grow in Idaho. This one, var. *montana* — photographed in the Clearwater Mountains—occurs from eastern Idaho and adjacent Montana to southeastern Oregon and south in the mountain states to New Mexico. A second, broad-leaf variety, var. *ovatum*, occurs further to the west and north.

**Silky lupine (left below)**
***Lupinus sericeus* Pursh**

The silky lupine is usually blue, but ranges in color from off-white to the intense blue shown here. It is mainly a foothills plant, growing no higher than the montane zone. It can be distinguished from *Lupinus argenteus* (following page) by its rounded leaflets, and a banner (the large upper petal) that is usually hairy on the back with a white center. The silky lupine was unknown to science until Meriwether Lewis collected a specimen on the Clearwater River in today's north-central Idaho on June 5, 1806.

It can be difficult to distinguish between *Lupinus sericeus* and *Lupinus argenteus*. The flower clusters of the former tend to be looser and are lower and extend well into the plant's leaves with the indvidual flowers smaller. The banners are often lighter or partially white. Both plants are variably hairy; *Lupinus sericeus* tends to be more so, and its calyx has a hump on the dorsal surface.

**Silver lupine**
***Lupinus argenteus* Pursh**
**var. *depressus*\***
**(Rydb.) C. L. Hitchc.**

Although the silver (or silvery) lupine is found in most states west of the Mississippi River, the variety shown here is restricted to the mountains of Idaho, Montana and Wyoming. It seldom grows more than a foot high and is quite at home at high elevations where, in August, alpine meadows are often covered with its bright flowers. It may be identified by this growth preference and by its crowded clusters of purple to blue flowers. *Lupinus argenteus* was unknown to science until the Lewis and Clark expedition returned a specimen (var. *argenteus*), collected in Montana, on July 7, 1806.

---

\*Recently, some have classified this plant as its own species, *Lupinus depressus* (the species name means "depressed" or "low").

### Longspur lupine
### *Lupinus arbustus* Douglas ex Lindl.
### var. *calcaratus* (Kellogg) S. L. Welsh

This plant, formerly classified as *Lupinus calcaratus* has recently been reclassified; *arbustus* means "small tree, or shrub" and *calcaratus* means "spurred" for a bump-like projection that extends backward from the top of the calyx. It is common in the Rocky Mountains and west to the coast, often growing in great profusion on sagebrush slopes as high as the subalpine zone. The color of the flowers varies considerably, from light purple to yellow—those shown here are typical.

### Stemless dwarf lupine
### *Lupinus lepidus* Douglas ex Lindl.
### var. *utahensis* (S. Watson) C. L. Hitchc.

This little lupine grows in the grass of montane meadows. Its flowers have short stems and the leaves, stems and base of the flowers are covered with long hairs giving the plant a furry, grayish appearance that helps to identify it.

*Lupinus lepidus* grows in Idaho, Oregon, Washington and, uncommonly, further north in British Columbia and Alaska. The name *lepidus*, from the Latin, means "neat" or "charming." A standardized common name, "elegant lupine," has been suggested for the plant.

### Long-stalked clover
### *Trifolium longipes* Nutt.

Several native clovers grow in our mountains. That shown on the left is the species most frequently seen at higher elevations, where it grows as high as the alpine zone. It is easily identified by its single small flowerhead atop a rather tall stem (*longipes,* means "long-stalked"). Close to a dozen varieties are recognized and their classification is based on minor technical differences. This plant's flowers are off-white, whereas in other varieties they may be purple. Its trifoliate leaves bear lance-shaped leaflets.

### Red clover
### *Trifolium pratense* L.

The red clover is an introduced species, useful both as a cultivated forage plant and as an ornamental. A Eurasian import, it is now well established throughout North America. The red clover is easily identified by its large trifoliate leaves, ovoid leaflets, and a large reddish-purple flower head. The species name, *pratense*, means "of the meadows." It is at home in our mountains, growing as high as the subalpine zone.

### White clover
### *Trifolium repens* L.

The white clover is another everywhere plant, introduced in the long-ago past; it grows in every state and province in North America. Its species name, "*repens*," is used fairly often as a species name for creeping plants (*cf.* "reptile") describing a tendency to grow along the ground. The trifoliate leaves are small and often form patches of considerable size in moist situations. It is seen, not uncommonly, growing in high mountain meadows.

### Purple-flowered woolly vetch
### *Vicia villosa* Roth

This purple flowered plant, also known as winter vetch, is a colorful native that is often seen growing near roadsides at higher elevations. It is villous (hairy) and its flowers grow in a spike-like cluster, always on one side of a tallish stem—an identifying feature. Another species of *Vicia*, the common vetch, or tare (*Vicia sativa* L.; not shown) is often seen near cultivated fields. It is characterized by large pink flowers, and dainty vine-like foliage whose pinnate leaves end in tendrils that clasp any nearby vegetation, commonly sagebrush in our area.

### Sainfoin
### *Onobrychis viciifolia* Scop.

Sainfoin is a European import whose usefulness as fodder has been known for millennia. In fact, the name *Onobrychis,* from the Greek, means "donkey-food." "Sainfoin," in turn, is derived from the French words *sain[t]* and *foin,* the latter word means "hay," thus "blessed hay." Its flowers are borne on a tall stem; its feathery leaves (*viciifolia* means "vetch-like leaves") have small, opposing leaflets. The flowers are small, but showy, with petals that are more prominently veined than those of any other member of the pea family in our area. Sainfoin, in profusion, occasionally turns montane hillsides pink.

### Yellow sweet-clover
### *Melilotus officinalis* (L.) Pall.

Although considered weeds, yellow sweet-clover and the very similar white sweet clover, *Melilotus alba* Medik. (not shown), were both introduced from Europe as fodder plants. They do have value, however, for they fix soil nitrogen. Their clover-like flowers and leaves are small. Sweet-clovers are extremely common along our roadsides, to mid-elevations. Homer used the word *melilotus* to describe animal fodder. Like many other imports in the pea family, sweet clovers are found everywhere in North America.

## Fumitory, or Bleeding Heart Family (Fumariaceae)

The fumitory family is not a large one, consisting of only 16 genera and 515 species. The name Fumariaceae is derived from that of a common European plant, *Fumaria officinalis*, found in the United States only as an ornamental plant, or garden escape. Members of the genus are known as "fumitories," a term that seems to have been derived from the latin terms *fumus* for "smoke" and *terrae* for "of the earth," possibly because the European plant has a wispy, amorphous growth pattern. Because the fumitory is little known here, the family is often referred to as the "bleeding heart family" for a plant well known to Americans. Flowers in this family are bilaterally symmetrical and four-petaled. Because the flowers often take unusual forms, the petals may be hard to delineate—as in the plants shown on the next two pages.

### Cusick's fitweed
### *Corydalis caseana* A. Gray var. *cusickii* (S. Watson) C. L. Hitchc.

Cusick's fitweed (or corydalis) is an uncommon, high montane to subalpine streamside plant that blooms in early summer. Its small flowers are unusual; an upper petal forms a long backward spur that extends as a hood over the front of the flower. This, joined to a lower petal, creates a flower tube that contains two darker inner petals. A tight cluster of fifty or so of these small purple flowers tops each stem. Its densely clustered flowers, its fern-like compound leaves, and its height make it an impressive plant. The genus is highly variable and several varieties are recognized; some are quite rare. The genus, in one or another of its varieties, is found in Idaho, Washington, Utah, New Mexico and—rarely—in Washington, Colorado and California. Sheep that graze on fitweeds die in convulsions, explaining its common name. Botanist Asa Gray named the species in 1874, giving it the species name *caseana*, to honor Eliphalet Lewis Case, (1843-1925), a California schoolteacher, Civil War veteran, and occasional plant collector who found the plant.

## Golden corydalis
### *Corydalis aurea* Willd.

The golden corydalis is an attractive sprawling plant with short-lived yellow flowers. It is occasionally encountered in our mountains, growing at least as high as the montane zone. Like other members of the genus, the golden corydalis can be identified by tubular flowers. Each contains two inner petals. One of the outer petals forms a fringed crest over the opening of the flower tube and extends backward to form a prominent spur. The plant's grayish-green leaves are basically pinnate, although the leaflets divide again (*i.e.*, they are "bipinnate"). Corydalises have exploding seed capsules that effectively broadcast many small seeds.

The golden corydalis grows in most of our western and northern tier states, and throughout Canada. Unusually, for such a wide-ranging plant, no subspecies or varieties are recognized. An inelegant standardized name, "scrambled eggs," has been proposed for the plant. *Corydalis* is the Greek name for the European crested lark; presumably attached to the flower because of its spur (analogous, perhaps, to "larkspur," the common name for the delphiniums), or possibly for the flower's prominent crest.

## Steer's head
### *Dicentra uniflora* Kellogg

This little plant, with horns formed by two upper petals, and an elongated head formed by two lower ones, is aptly named. It blooms early in the spring at montane to subalpine elevations. Steer's heads are not rare they are elusive. Look for them on rocky hillsides below snowline. They are small and often grow in sagebrush, so finding one is usually a matter of chance. A similar plant (*Dicentra pauciflora*) with shorter horns grows in California, so ours is sometimes known as the "long-horned steer's head."

Several other unusual wildflowers (not shown here) also belong to *Dicentra*. These include bleeding heart (*Dicentra formosa* (Haw.) Walp.) and dutchman's breeches (*Dicentra cucullaria* [L.] Bern.) Both are native to the Northwest and both are used as ornamental plants.

## Gentian Family (Gentianaceae)

Gentians are the aristocrats of alpine flowers. Finding a patch of bright blue gentians blooming at summer's end is ample reward for climbing high. Many gentians favor moist, rich soil deposited on the banks of slow flowing streams, along the shores of mountain lakes, and in wet mountain meadows. Late-blooming gentians are tolerant of cold, and may continue to flower even when the nights are freezing, for they are low to the ground and sheltered by sun-warmed earth—microclimate is everything for mountain flowers. Gentians have been so-named for more than two millenia. King Gentius in the second century BC ruled Illyria, a Balkan country. The king believed that the bitter roots of a certain flowering plant had medicinal value. He was wrong, but the plant has been associated with his name ever since, and so we have "gentian" today. The family is made up of 79 genera and about 1,270 species. Most are found in the north temperate zone; a half-dozen or so are cultivated as ornamental plants. Species belonging to at least five genera, *Gentianopsis, Gentiana, Gentianella, Swertia,* and *Frasera* grow in the mountains of Idaho. Typically their flowers are symmetrical; their leaves are opposed. The petals are joined at the base to form trumpet, urn-shaped or salverform blooms; *Gentianopsis* and *Frasera* flowers have four petals, and other genera have five.

## Pleated gentian
### *Gentiana affinis* Griseb.

The pleated gentian takes its common name from an inward folding membrane that joins one petal to the next. As in this plant, the petals often have a reticulated pattern of greenish spots on their upper surfaces. Pleated gentians spread by sending out roots, and are often found growing in clusters that sometimes suggest the "fairy rings" formed by proliferating field mushrooms. Each of the pleated gentian's stems bears several pairs of small, opposite, lanceolate leaves and a terminal flower. As with other members of this genus, this gentian prefers moist montane meadows and the banks of lakes and streams. The pleated gentian is a well-distributed species, found throughout the western United States and across Canada to Ontario.

## Explorer's gentian
### *Gentiana calycosa* Griseb.

The explorer's gentian (known also as the the mountain gentian or bog gentian) is the largest, showiest, highest, and latest blooming of our gentians. It grows close to treeline, in moist subalpine meadows and on the loamy banks of slow-flowing streams. It sometimes blooms well into September, accompanied only by lingering asters and the ubiquitous yarrow. Its flowers are five-petaled, speckled inside and, like the plant shown above, have a "pleat" connecting the petals. The leaves tend to be wider than those of our other *Gentiana*. Its species name, *calycosa,* from the Latin word for "calyx," refers in this case to the cup-shaped flowers. The explorer's gentian is found in most of the western states and Canadian provinces.

## One-flowered gentian
### *Gentianopsis simplex* (A. Gray) Iltis

The one-flowered gentian has a small and—as its name suggests—a plain flower, noticeable mostly for its intense blue color. Until recently classified in genus *Gentiana*, it is now in *Gentianopsis*, a genus made up of similar four-petaled gentians. It is a close relative of the Rocky Mountain fringed gentian (*Gentianopsis thermalis* [Kuntze] Iltis., not shown), a plant that also grows in Idaho. Both have four petals, but this one usually has little, if any, fringing at the end of the petals. Both plants grow along streams, and in moist high montane to subalpine meadows, blooming from mid-July through August. The ending of the generic name, *-opsis,* is derived from the Greek word for "view" or "looks like," thus "a plant that looks like (or is similar to) a gentian." The species is found in Idaho, west to the coastal states (except Washington), and rarely in Montana and Wyoming.

### Clustered elkweed (above)
### *Frasera fastigiata* (Pursh) A. Heller

The clustered elkweed is found from Idaho to Latah counties in northern Idaho and in the nearby Blue Mountains of Oregon and Washington. It is a tall, large-leaved plant topped with four-petaled blue flowers. It is the only member of the gentian family that Meriwether Lewis collected (June 14th, 1806) on the Weippe Prairie. The name, *fastigiata*, implies "cone-like" for the shape of the flower cluster.

### White gentian (above)
### *Frasera montana* Mulford

The white gentian is found in central Idaho north of Galena Summit (US Highway 75). A high montane plant, it blooms in late spring on dry ground, usually in the company of sagebrush. Four-petaled, clustered flowers and white bordered, narrow leaves help to identify it.

### Monument plant
### *Frasera speciosa* Douglas ex Griseb.

The monument plant (giant frasera, green gentian) is a tall, narrow, cone-shaped plant with flowers clustered around the upper part of its stem. The plants live for many years, but bloom only once and then die. Flowering is unpredictable, but seems related to moisture. The flowers are about 3/4" diameter with long sepals visible between each of its four purple-spotted petals. Each petal has two pits at its base and four stamens surrounding a one-seed ovary. The name *Frasera* honors John Fraser, (1750-1811), a Scots nurseryman who collected in south-eastern North America. The name *speciosa* means "showy." The plant grows throughout the western United States.

**Autumn dwarf-gentian**
*Gentianella amarella* (L.) Boerner

**Swertia**
*Swertia perennis* L.

This is the daintiest of our Gentianaceae. It flowers during the second half of August in moist, high montane to subalpine meadows. With minor differences, the same plant ranges across North America, Europe and Asia. Our plants are pink, but in other places they may be off-white or even pale yellow. They may be identified by the fringe of fine hairs inside the petals—shown clearly in the magnified view above. The species name *amarella* means "a little bitter."

The swertia (also felwort or star gentian) is the only member of its genus found in America. It is a late-blooming circumboreal plant found in all of the western states, in British Columbia, and in Eurasia. The plant favors wet montane to subalpine meadows. Its four petals range in color from light purple to almost black, each petal has two nectar pits at its base. The fruiting capsule is quite prominent. Emanuel Sweert (1552-1612), was a Dutch botanist who composed a catalog of plants.

## Geranium Family (Geraniaceae)

The geranium family consists of five genera and 760 species. The name is derived from the Greek word *geranos*, meaning "crane," referring to the long pointed beak formed by the style as the seeds form. Perversely, the popular and attractive garden "geranium" does not belong to the genus *Geranium* at all, but to *Pelargonium*, a genus made up of almost 300 tropical plants found mostly in South Africa. The economic importance of the family is due entirely to the popularity of its cultivated ornamental varieties. Those in genus *Geranium* differ from the pelargoniums by the symmetrical configuration of their flowers, with five sepals, five petals, ten stamens and a five part pistil and their (usually) pink to purple coloration. As many as ten species of *Geranium* grow in the Northwest, but of all of these, only two are native species.

## Sticky geranium
### *Geranium viscosissimum*
### Fisch. & C. A. Mey.

The sticky geranium flowers from spring until nearly summer's end. The flowers are usually pink with deep red to purple veins, although their color varies from almost white to light purple. Deeply cut compound leaves are a distinguishing feature. The plants prefer, but are not restricted to moist and shady areas; they grow as high as the subalpine zone where the plants grow close to the ground. The leaves and stems are sticky explaining both common and scientific names. The very similar white geranium, *Geranium richardsonii* Fisch. & Trautv. (not shown), also a native species, grows in a like environment further north in Idaho than this plant. Both are found throughout the West.

## Crane's bill
### *Erodium cicutarium*
### L'Hér. ex Aiton

The crane's bill (also stork's bill, and filaree) is a small, pink-flowered Eurasian plant that now has spread worldwide. In early spring the plants often appear in great numbers. Although considered a weed, the erodium is an excellent browse plant. It grows as high as the montane zone, although the plants are less common there than at lower elevations. Crane's bills are creeping plants, usually only an inch or so high. Their long, persistent styles explains the erodium's scientific and common names (*Erodium* from the Greek means "crane" or "heron"). The species name, *cicutarium* implies that its leaves resemble those of the *Cicuta*, the European water hemlock.

## Currant Family (Grossulariaceae)

The Currant Family is a small one, consisting of only one genus and about 200 species. In the past, currants and gooseberries were included in the Saxifrage family, but are now in their own own family, Grossulariaceae. The currants (*Ribes*) and the gooseberries (*Grossularia*) were also classified as two separate genera, but the plants are so similar that both are now included in a single genus, *Ribes* (pronounced "RIBE-eez," from an Arabic word that means "acidic"). The main difference between currants and gooseberries is that the former have prickly ("armed") stems, whereas currants are smooth-stemmed. All members of the currant family are shrubs that bear (mostly) edible berries. The garden gooseberry (*Ribes uva-crispa*) and the cultivated currant (*Ribes nigra*) have been grown for centuries. Many wild species of *Ribes* grow in our mountains and they resemble each other—and the domesticated fruit—to the point that if one is acquainted with one species it is not difficult to recognize others as members of the same family.

### Golden currant
### *Ribes aureum* Pursh

The golden current grows in all but our southeastern states. It is identified by its yellow flowers, three-lobed leaves, and tasty berries. While all *Ribes* are to a degree edible, the golden currant is the sweetest. The Lewis and Clark expedition first collected the plant near the Three Forks of the Missouri on July 29, 1805, and again the following spring near today's The Dalles on the Columbia River (April 16, 1805).

### Squawberry
### *Ribes cereum* Douglas

The squawberry, or wax current, grows as high as treeline in our western states, and east to South Dakota and Oklahoma. Its creamy-white flowers are about half an inch long, and its translucent berries are edible, but tasteless. Indians used the fruit for pemmican, hence the plant's common name. David Douglas was the first to collect this species along the Columbia River in 1825. The name *cereum* means "waxy" for the berries' appearance.

### Swamp Black Gooseberry
### *Ribes lacustre* (Pers.) Poir.

The prickly wild gooseberrry is another easily identified *Ribes*. It grows in moist places and on streambanks. The small, filmy flowers and shiny leaves are distinctive. Its stems are prickly. The plants black fruit may also have soft prickles, unlike those of other wild currants. The berries are edible but sour—only suitable as an emergency food.

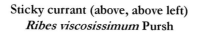

### Sticky currant (above, above left)
### *Ribes viscosissimum* Pursh

Touch this plant's foliage and you will see how it got its names. Meriwether Lewis collected the plant—unknown then to science—on June 16, 1806, on the Lolo Trail while eastward bound, noting that it grew on "The hights of the rocky mountain...Fruit indifferent and gummy..." The plant is common in our western states and adjacent Canadian provinces.

### Hudson's Bay currant
### (center left, below left)
### *Ribes hudsonianum* Richards.

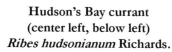

The Hudson's Bay currant (also northern black currant) is a montane to subalpine streamside plant, that grows all across northern North America. The shrubs bear sprays of white flowers that ripen into black fruit. Maple-like leaves give off an acrid odor similar to that of cat urine, explaining another common name, "stinking currant." Despite this, the berries are reasonably palatable. Two varieties occur in Idaho; ours is var. *petiolare* (Dougl.) Jancz.; the other, var. *hudsonianum*, grows near the Canadian border.

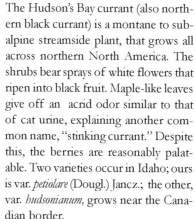

### Henderson's gooseberry
### *Ribes oxyacanthoides* L. var. *hendersonii*
### (C. L. Hitchc.) P. K. Holmgren

Henderson's gooseberry is an alpine plant that grows in Idaho's Lost River Range (where this plant was photographed), and in Montana's Anaconda, and Nevada's Toiyabe mountain ranges. Although it lacks small branch prickles, it is armed with impressively long thorns. We have not seen a fruiting plant. Several other varieties of *Ribes oxyacanthoides* are recognized; these occur at lower elevations. The species as a whole is found from Alaska to Hudson's Bay, south to the Great Lakes and northern Great Plains. Louis Fourniquet Henderson (1853-1942), for whom this variety was named, was Professor of Botany at the University of Idaho and, subsequently, at the University of Oregon, during the first half of the twentieth century.

# Hydrangea Family (Hydrangeaceae)

The Hydrangeaceae, a small family, consists of sixteen genera and about 250 species. Most grow in the north temperate zone. The family's chief economic importance lies in various plants that are cultivated as ornamental trees and shrubs—probably the best known are species of *Hydrangea* and the mock oranges (*Philadelphus* spp.). Only one member of the family, *Philadelphus lewisii*—Idaho's state flower—is native to Idaho. While Idahoans universally refer to the plant as the "syringa," more correctly it should be known as Lewis's mock-orange. It is an attractive, fragrant, white-flowered shrub or small tree that was unknown to science until Meriwether Lewis collected two specimens on the expedition's return trip in 1806. We do not know how the plant came to be known as a syringa; seemingly it was confused with the common lilac, *Syringa vulgaris*, a member of the olive family (Oleaceae).

Recent DNA studies suggest that the Hydrangeaceae family is related to the Cornaceae, the dogwood family.

### Lewis's mock orange
### *Philadelphus lewisii* Pursh

Meriwether Lewis collected the mock-orange on today's Clearwater River on May 6, 1806, and again on July 4, 1806, on today's Bitterroot River. He noted, correctly, that the plant might be a *Philadelphus*. Syringas, as the plants are known in Idaho, are not hard to identify, for their fragrant flowers set them apart from the western dogwood, the only other tree with four-petaled flowers (the dogwood's "petals" are actually bracts) with which it might be confused. Apparently the mock orange was more common when Lewis found the plant than it is today. It still grows along the Clearwater, but in reduced numbers.

The generic name, *Philadelphus*, was derived from two Greek words, *philos* for "love" and *adelphos* meaning "brother." It is said to have been derived from the name of Ptolemy Philadelphus, an Egyptian king (283-247 B.C.).

## Waterleaf Family (Hydrophyllaceae)

*Hydrophyllum* in Latin means "water-leaf," and it is from that word that this family's name was derived. The original waterleaf was a European plant represented in antiquity by an "ornament used in sculptured capitals, supposed to be a conventionalized representation of the leaf of some aquatic plant" (OED). Linnaeus appropriated the name *Hydrophyllum* and applied it to our plant probably without realizing that Hydrophyllaceae are found only in the New World. It is a relatively small family made up of 15 genera and about 300 species. Its members are in many ways similar to those in the Borage (Forget-me-not) family—so much so that some taxonomists lump the two families together as Boraginaceae. Hydrophyllaceae are found throughout the American West and are strongly represented in the Northwest. Several have been cultivated as ornamental garden varieties (primarily species of *Phacelia*), the family's only economic importance. Typically, flowers of the waterleaf family have five sepals and five petals that are united at their base to form small bell- or saucer-shaped flowers. These may be solitary or form clusters (including fiddlehead shaped "helicoid cymes").

### Dwarf hesperochiron
### *Hesperochiron pumilus*
### (Douglas ex Griseb.) Porter

The dwarf hesperochiron is a pretty little plant, with white, loosely clustered, veined flowers. It is so unlike other members of the water-leaf family that when first seen, often in the company of spring-beauties (*Claytonia* spp.), one may have trouble placing it. The plants bloom in the spring on ground still moist from the snow-melt. The word *Hesperochiron* is derived from *hesperius* ("western"), and *Chiron*, the name of a mythological centaur. The significance of the name is unknown, possibly it was attached to a similar plant in antiquity. The species name, *pumilus* means "dwarf" in Latin. The plant grows in all of the western states.

### Ballhead waterleaf
### *Hydrophyllum capitatum*
### Douglas ex Benth.

The ballhead waterleaf is an early spring blooming plant found along seasonal freshets or on slopes still moist from the snowmelt. Attractive, round, frizzy, purple flowerheads up to two inches in diameter soon appear, partially hidden by the plant's bright green, incised leaves. The small flowers have five sepals, five petals, and five projecting anthers. Typically purple, the flowers may range to white at subalpine elevations. There are several varieties of the waterleaf distinguished chiefly by the length of the leaf and flower stems. The plants are found in the four states of the Northwest, south to Colorado and Utah, and north to British Columbia and Alberta.

### Purple-fringe *Phacelia sericea* (Graham) A. Gray

The purple-fringe is one of our more spectacular alpine flowers. It blooms in early to mid-summer on the banks of high mountain lakes and in moist open areas on ridges, where nearby snow-banks and cornices are still melting. The species name, *sericea*, means "silky" for the hairs on the foliage. Two varieties are recognized; ours is var. *sericea*. A larger variety, *Phacelia sericea* var. *ciliosa* Rydb., also grows in Idaho at lower elevations although we have not encountered the plant. The purple-fringe is distributed throughout the West, and north to Alaska.

*Phacelia* is a large genus (about 150 species) well represented in Idaho and surrounding states. Many, like the purple-fringe, are showy plants.

129

### Silverleaf phacelia
### *Phacelia hastata* Douglas ex Lehm.

*Phacelia*, from the Greek *phakelos*, means "bundle," for the clustered flowers common to this genus; *hastata* means "spear-shaped" for the plant's (inconstant) pointed lower leaves with small lateral lobes. Tightly coiled helicoid cymes are prominent. At lower altitudes, silverleaf phacelias are tall and the flowers are white-petaled (left). Higher up, they tend to be purple-flowered (right). Higher still, as alpine plants, they hug the ground (as in the illustrations above) and are sometimes classified as var. *alpina* (Rydb.) Cronquist. Silverleaf phacelieas are common plants found almost everywhere in the West. A similar plant, *Phacelia heterophylla* (not shown), grows at lower elevations.

### Franklin's phacelia
### *Phacelia franklinii* (R. Br.) A. Gray

The five-petaled, light purple flowers of Franklin's phacelia bloom as a scorpioid cyme in common with many other plants in the waterleaf family. Its leaves are pinnate with blunt lobes. The plants may have only a single stem, but more commonly there is a central stem with several smaller ones surrounding it to form a clump. The species name, *franklinii*, honors Sir John Franklin (1786-1847), an ill-fated explorer of northern North America and the Arctic who died while searching for a Northwest Passage. John Richardson (1787-1865), a physician-naturalist with Franklin's first expedition, collected this plant (and several others shown in this book) in northern Saskatchewan in 1820 and named it for the expedition's leader. Franklin's phacelia ranges northward from the mountains of Utah, and Wyoming, through the American Northwest to Alaska and as far east as Manitoba.

### Idaho phacelia
### *Phacelia idahoensis* L.E. Hend.

The Idaho phacelia is a tall plant whose purple flowers are borne on a spike-like stem. As with other phacelias, the flowers are on coiled stemlets that gradually unroll and are responsible for the common name "scorpionweed" sometimes used for plants in this genus. Some species of phacelia are quite localized in their distribution. This is true of *Phacelia idahoensis* found only in the central counties of Idaho (this plant was photographed in Custer County, west of Stanley). The ending *-ensis* used with a species name has the meaning of "originating in."

### Thread-leaf phacelia
### *Phacelia linearis* (Pursh) Holz.

The thread-leaf phacelia bears showy, pink to light-purple flowers. Typically it is found in foothills and at lower elevations in the mountains. It is a rather common late-spring to early-summer plant that favors dry surroundings where hairy leaves serve to conserve moisture. The leaves, while narrow, hardly seem narrow enough to deserve the name "thread-leaf." Unlike the Idaho phacelia shown above, *Phacelia linearis* is common in the western provinces and states, east of the Cascade and Sierra Nevada ranges. Meriwether Lewis collected this plant, then new to science, on the expedition's return trip, at today's The Dalles, Oregon, on April 17, 1806.

# Mint Family (Lamiaceae)

The Mint Family, Lamiaceae (an older family name, Labiatae, is also correct) consists of approximately 265 genera and 6,000 species. Its members typically have square stems and many produce volatile oils responsible for their "minty" odor. Characteristically, the flowers are borne in whorls ("verticillasters") above paired, usually toothed leaves. The flowers are irregular with five petals, two of which form an upper "lip"—explaining the older family name (*labiatus* means "lip-shaped" in Latin). While not all species share the above characteristics, there usually is little problem in identifying members of the family. It includes ornamental garden plants (*Salvia*, bee-balms [*Monarda*], and others) as well as many useful herbs: garden mints (*Mentha* spp.) such as peppermint, spearmint, catnip, etc., lavender (*Lavendula*), various garden sages (*Salvia* spp.), as well as other culinary herbs including species of thyme (*Thymus*), oregano and marjoram (*Oreganum*), basil (*Ocimum*), rosemary (*Rosemarinum*), California's yerba buena (*Satureja douglasii* Benth.), and the list goes on. About two dozen genera grow in the Northwest including the fragrant native field mint, *Mentha arvense* L., often found in Idaho growing in moist places at lower elevations. Several Eurasian members of the family have also found a home in our Northwest.

### Western horsemint
### *Agastache urticifolia* (Benth.) Kuntze

The western horsemint (or giant hyssop) grows in great numbers along our mountain trails, especially in areas that retain moisture from the snow-melt. It occurs in all of the states contiguous to Idaho, as well as California and Colorado, growing as high as the subalpine zone. The tall, square-stemmed plants have a pronounced minty odor. *Agastache,* derived from two Greek words, implies "a spike of wheat" reflecting the form of the flowerhead. The Latin-derived species name, *urticifolia,* means "nettle-leaved" for the resemblance of the plant's leaves to those of the common stinging nettle (*Urtica dioica*).

### Snapdragon skullcap, *Scutellaria antirrhinoides* Benth.

Although scutellarias do not smell minty and do not resemble garden mint, their irregular, bilaterally symmetrical flowers and square stems suggest that they are, in fact, in the mint family, Lamiaceae. This plant is found in Idaho and west to the coastal states. A look-alike, although somewhat larger plant, the narrow-leaved skullcap, *Scutellaria angustifolia* Pursh (not shown) grows a bit further north. The name "skullcap" was derived from the shape of the calyx, fancied to resemble a visored helmet in some species. Similarly, the prominent bump on the calyx was thought to resemble a tray (Latin *scutella*) and *antirrhinoides* means "snapdragon-like" for its resemblance to that flower (the two plants are not related).

## Flax Family (Linaceae)

The flax family is not a large one. It consists of eight genera and about 250 species. It is represented in our mountains by only one native plant, Lewis's wild blue flax, *Linum lewisii*. The almost identical common, or domestic flax, *Linum usitatissimum*, occurs in settled areas both as an ornamental and as a garden escape. Both wild and cultivated flax are closely related to the Eurasian wild flax, *Linum perenne*, the presumed ancestor of the domestic plant. As an indication of how closely related these three plants are, some classify our wild flax, *Linum lewisii*, as a subspecies of the Eurasian plant.

Flax has been an important source of fiber and oil since prehistoric times, evidenced by remnants of linen found in Swiss lake dwellings and in ancient Egyptian tombs. Flax is grown commercially today, both for its fiber (although linen has now been largely replaced by synthetic fibers) and for its seed. Flaxseed (or linseed) is about 40% oil by weight; it is of great importance to the paint industry. Additionally, flaxseed and flaxseed oil are being used increasingly as dietary supplements and in health foods. In the past, flaxseed poultices were in common use—a favored means of applying heat topically to injured or diseased parts of the body.

**Wild blue flax**
***Linum lewisii* Pursh var. *alpicola* Jepson**

The wild blue flax (Lewis's blue flax, prairie flax), *Linum lewisii*, is widely distributed west of the Mississippi River, north to Alaska. Two varieties are recognized. The variety shown here occurs in circumscribed islands in the mountains of central Idaho as well as in Nevada and California. The plants grow on rocky, south-facing slopes, blooming from June to August, according to elevation—we have seen them in a reduced form well above tree-line. The flowers of this variety are a light grayish-blue, unlike the deep blue of plants (var. *lewisii*) that grow at lower elevations. The species name honors Meriwether Lewis who collected the previously unknown wild blue flax on Montana's Sun River during the expedition's return journey (July 9, 1806). It is one of four plants that bear the explorer's name.* A yellow-petaled species, the Uinta mountain (or sandplain) flax, *Linum kingii* S. Watson, occurs in south-eastern Idaho, and elsewhere in the Great Basin drainage, although we have not encountered it.

---

\* The other three are: bitterroot, *Lewisia rediviva*, mock-orange (syringa), *Philadelphus lewisii*; and Lewis's monkeyflower, *Mimulus lewisii*.

**Cultivated flax**
***Linum usitatissimum* L.**

Cultivated, or garden flax, is commonly planted as an ornamental, both in gardens, and as a roadside plant where it often forms crowded masses of bright blue flowers. These are annuals plants—unlike the perennial wild blue flax—that reseed themselves and may persist for years in the same location. There are other differences between the wild and cultivated plants. The wild flax has slightly wider leaves and the alpine variety described above is lighter in color. Also, the cultivated flax is dimorphic in that some flowers have anthers that are longer than the styles, and in other flowers the opposite is true. The species name, *usitatissimum* means "most useful." Forms of this plant are cultivated both for fiber and for linseed (flaxseed) oil.

## Blazing-star Family (Loasaceae)

The blazing star family is small, made up of twenty genera and about 320 species. It is represented in Idaho by species of *Mentzelia* that grow to the montane zone or higher in our mountains. The family has little economic importance other than the occasional use of some of the plants as cultivated ornamentals. As with various evening primroses (Onagraceae), the flowers open in the evening, are pollinated by night-flying insects, and then fade during the day.

### Ten-petaled blazing star
### *Mentzelia decapetala*
### (Pursh) Urban & Gilg ex Gilg

The ten-petaled blazing star is not a flower easily missed. It blooms late in the day, is moth-pollinated at night, and closes early in the morning. During the rest of the day the plants look like tall, rough-leaved weeds. The ten-petaled flowers include five true petals and five inner modified stamens ("staminodes"). Lewis and Clark collected this new-to-science plant in August, 1804, near today's Homer, Nebraska. Primarily a Great Plains plant, it grows from the Mississippi River west to Idaho where it is occurs in scattered locations, growing on south-facing gravelly slopes to fairly high elevations.

### Blazing star
### *Mentzelia laevicaulis*
### (Douglas ex Hook.) Torr. & A. Gray

This plant, usually known simply as the blazing star, is relatively tall with rough foliage. Five of its many stamens are flattened and petaloid, but not nearly as large as its five true petals. It grows in Montana, Wyoming and Colorado, west to British Columbia and the three coastal states. The plants are often seen growing on gravelly road embankments, as high as the subalpine zone. Because the flowers of these two mentzelias are showy they are sometimes cultivated as garden ornamentals in dry environments. The genus is named for German botanist, Christian Mentzel (1622-1701).

# Mallow Family (Malvaceae)

The mallow family is a moderately large one of approximately 197 genera and 2,850 species worldwide. It takes its name from the Latin word *malva*, used in the past for various mallows. The family has considerable economic importance. *Gossypium* species include cotton plants, important for their textile fiber and for oil extracted from their seeds. Species of hibiscus and the related rose-of-sharon (*Hibiscus* spp.) are ornamental garden plants. Okra (*Abelmoschus esculentus* (L) Moench) is also a Malvaceae. The hollyhock (*Alcea rosea* L) is another popular garden mallow. Most mallows are easily recognizable. Their flowers are five-petaled and grow in terminal clusters. "Staminate tubes" formed by fusion of the filaments of the anthers protrude from the center of the flowers (very noticeable in the hibiscus, but present in all) and help with identification.

### Streambank globe mallow
### *Iliamna rivularis* (Douglas ex Hook.) Greene

This mallow is sometimes referred to as a wild hollyhock although hollyhocks are a species of *Alcea*, a genus that does not grow in our area. The name *Iliamna* apparently came from an Athabaskan word, used for Lake Iliamna in Alaska; *rivularis*, means "of brooklets." The latter is an apt term, for this lovely montane plant blooms in mid-summer along streams, and in dry creek beds. Its showy pink flowers, the flowers' staminate tubes, and alternating maple-like leaves identify the plant. The streambank globe mallow is found mostly in the western mountains states.

### Gooseberryleaf globe mallow
### *Sphaeralcea grossulariifolia* (Hook. & Arn.) Rydb.

This plant is sometimes considered a weed because of its casual growth along trails and roadsides. If one believes that weeds are competitive, harmful plants then this plant is getting a bad press. It is non-aggressive and its five-petaled orange flowers brighten the landscape. The plant grows only in Rocky Mountain and Pacific coastal states. The Greek *sphaera* means "globe" and *alcea* is the name for the hollyhock. The species name *grossulariifolia* is also from the Latin and means "gooseberry leafs," from the similarity of this plant's leaves to those of the common gooseberry.

### Oregon checkermallow
### *Sidalcea oregona* (Nutt. ex Torr. & A. Gray) A. Gray
### var. *oregana.*

Flowers in the mallow family are often quite showy. This plant, common in Idaho, is an example. It is tall with veined, light pinkish-to-purple flowers borne in spike-like clusters ("racemes"). Its alternate leaves are made up of deeply dissected narrow leaflets. The species is quite variable and half a dozen or more varieties are recognized. *Sidalcea oregona* is found in Idaho and surrounding states (although rare in Montana and British Columbia) and in California. It is often seen along roadsides, in moist meadows and with sagebrush, where it blooms in mid-summer. The generic name, *Sidalcea*, was derived from the names of two European mallows: hollyhock (*alcea*) and *sida* (the latter is the fanpetal plant).

### Common mallow, *Malva sylvestris* L.

True mallows—species of *Malva*—are Eurasian plants. Several came with settlers to the New World centuries ago and are now quite at home in North America. The common mallow, shown on the left, would certainly place high on anyone's list of showy weeds; it resembles a small hollyhock with attractive, purple-streaked, five-petaled flowers. More common in the Pacific coastal states, it is now sometimes found at higher elevations in Idaho. While Americans do not recognize it as a food plant, its leaves have long been used as greens, both raw and cooked.

Similarly, the leaves and the small button, or cheese-shaped, fruit of two common plants, the cheeseweeds (*Malva parviflora* L., *Malva neglecta* Wallr.; neither are shown here) are quite edible—these small, white-to pink-flowered weeds commonly invade gardens, and disturbed soil throughout North America. Their foliage is succulent and the uncooked leaves impart a slippery sensation to the tongue—not surprising given their family relationship to okra (*Abelmoschus esculenta*).

## Water-lily Family (Nymphaeaceae)

The water-lily family is small, consisting of only six genera and about 65 species. It is a primitive family of considerable taxonomic interest as its members are believed to represent relics of early plant forms that preceded the development of monocotyledonous plants and then persisted by adapting successfully to a fully aquatic existence. Various species and their hybrids have been grown for millennia as ornamentals. This is the family's chief economic importance, although the seeds of several species are used elsewhere for food; those of some are said to have narcotic properties. South American species of *Victoria* (named in honor of the English monarch), noted for their enormous floating leaves and fragrant flowers, are the most spectacular members of the family.

**Rocky Mountain pond-lily, *Nuphar polysepala* Engelm.**

The Rocky Mountain pond-lily is a wide-ranging plant that grows in quiet ponds well up into the mountains. As with other members of the family, the pond-lilies have bulky roots; stems with specialized air pockets, and large fruiting bodies whose seeds were used as food by Native Americans. The thick yellow sepals, small hidden petals, and ball-like shape of the flower are typical of the genus. Members are sometimes used as easily grown ornamentals in water gardens. This species grows as far north as Alaska and the Northwest Territories of Canada, and south to California, Arizona and New Mexico.

# Evening Primrose Family (Onagraceae)

The evening primrose family consists of seventeen genera and 650 species. Although representatives are found world-wide, they are especially abundant in the Americas. Plants from several genera are cultivated as garden ornamentals, examples include North American species of *Clarkia, Epilobium, Gaura* and *Ludwigia,* as well as cultivars of *Fuchsia* from Central and South America. The family's flowers are radially symmetrical with four petals, four sepals and four, or occasionally eight, stamens. In many species, the petals and sepals are joined into a long narrow tube that looks more like a stem than part of the flower. The Onagraceae are well represented in our mountains, especially by *Epilobium* species at higher elevations. The common name, "evening primrose family," reflects the tendency of various short-blooming flowers in this family to open in the afternoon and fade away the following day, an understandable trait when one learns that they depend on night-flying moths for pollination. It is interesting that many of the species that flower only for an evening open suddenly, often in a matter of seconds. Most bear long "strings" of pollen that are picked up by nectar-gathering moths and carried from one flower to the next.

## Northern suncup
### *Camissonia subacaulis*
### (Pursh) P. H. Raven

The northern suncup (also long-leaf evening primrose) is a low-growing, four-petaled summer plant found only on moist ground. The name, *subacaulis*, means "not much of a stem," referring to the flowers, for as with many members of this family, the flower's "stem" is actually part of the flower tube and the actual stem is very short. Its wide leaves are said to be edible greens. The plant ranges from the northern Rockies, west to central Washington and eastern California. It was first collected by Meriwether Lewis on the Weippe Prairie in northern Idaho on June 14, 1806. The generic name has varied back and forth between *Oenothera* and *Camissonia*, the latter is now preferred. The name honors German botanist, novelist, and composer Adelbert von Chamisso (1781-1838) a member of the Russian Kotzebue Pacific expedition of 1815-1818.

## Tansy-leaved suncup
### *Camissonia tanacetifolia*
### (Torr. & A. Gray) P. H. Raven

The tansy-leaved suncup's growth habit is similar to that of the plant shown above and it has a similar range, although, in Idaho at least, it seems to be less common. It is characterized by pinnate leaves that are rather like those of the common tansy (*Tanacetum vulgare*) explaining both its common and scientific species names.

**Fireweed (left to right above)**
*Chamerion angustifolium*
**(L.) Holub**

Because the common fireweed prefers disturbed ground, it is considered a weed, an undeserved reputation, at least in our mountains. It spreads by underground stems, reclaiming ground after wildfires. As reforestation proceeds, fireweeds are replaced by other flora. Look at its flowers and you'll see that it is an attractive plant. Four-petaled flowers and a stem-like flower tube are family characteristics. The tube contains the ovary; this matures into a long pod-like seed capsule. The chamerions shown here grow across North America (except in a few southern states) and in Eurasia. They have recently been reclassified from genus *Epilobium* to *Chamerion*, a pre-Linnaean name for the fireweed (or rosebay willow-weed as it is known in Europe). Ours is the common hairy phase found in most of North America, var. *canescens* (Alph. Wood) N. H. Holmgren & P. K. Holmgren.

### Red willow-herb
### *Chamerion latifolium* (L.) Holub (left)

The willow-herbs are named for the resemblance of their leaves to those of the willows. The willow-herbs shown here are both summer-blooming plants; both grow as high as the subalpine zone. The red (or dwarf) willow-herb is found only on the sandy banks and sandbars of mountain streams. It is a lovely flower whose four red petals alternate with color-matched, lanceolate sepals. The name, *latifolium*, means "wide leaf" although the leaves are wide only in comparison to those of the fireweed shown above.

### Ragged robin
### *Clarkia pulchella* Pursh

The ragged robin (also known by many other common names including the now preferred "pink-fairies") is a plant of the Northwest, best seen growing wild. The plant is pretty much localized to where Meriwether Lewis collected it near today's Kamiah, Idaho, on June 1, 1806. It was, as Lewis recognized, an odd little plant, then unknown to science. It is interesting both for its unusual appearance, and also because it is the only plant of those that the expedition collected that bears William Clark's name. This plant defined the genus *Clarkia*. Now about forty species of *Clarkia* are recognized.

### Rock-fringe
### *Epilobium obcordatum* A. Gray

Finding unexpected blooms in inhospitable places is one of the alpine hiker's great pleasures. So it is with the rock-fringe (also known as the rose willow-herb), a showy, bright pink plant that flowers in July and into August. While native to mountains in Oregon, California, Nevada and Idaho, it is quite localized in its growth preference. The rock-fringe is a subalpine plant that grows in rocky crevices, or at the base of south-facing rocks and cliffs. The plants are small-leaved creepers. Its flowers are large—up to two inches in diameter—with four, bright pink, heart-shaped (*obcordatum*) petals, eight stamens and a long dependent style tipped with a cross-shaped stigma.

The generic name, *Epilobium*, was derived from the long, stem-like flower tube which contains the ovary (*epi-* means "on" and *-lobos* refers to the ovary), visible in these flowers and those of the epilobiums shown on the following page.

### Autumn willow-weed
### *Epilobium brachycarpum* C. Presl

The autumn willow-weed is a mid- to high altitude plant that blooms in August. It is a common, spindly, windblown plant that grows on bare, dry ground. Its many tiny pink to white flowers have four deeply notched petals lined with reddish veins. If you try to photograph the plant you will find that it is in constant motion, waving with the slightest breeze. Formerly classified as *Epilobium paniculatum* Nutt. ex Torr. & A. Gray, its new species name, *brachycarpum,* means "short-fruit."

### Alpine willow-weed
### *Epilobium lactiflorum* Hausskn.

The four-petaled flowers of the alpine willowweed are tiny, as is the plant overall. Until recently its species name was *Epilobium alpinum* L., but because of confusion with other species of the same name, it has been reclassified as *Epilobium lactiflorum.* Its species name is derived from the Latin *lacteus* for milky and *-florus* for flowered. Both the scientific and common names are misleading, however, for this plant's flowers range in color from pure white through white with pink veins (as in the one shown here), to fully pink or even rose. It is wide-ranging, found throughout the western United States, and north to Alaska. It also grows in Maine, in the northeastern Canadian provinces and east to Greenland and Eurasia. Any small white to pink, high ranging *Epilobium* with slightly serrated leaves will most likely be this plant.

### Common willow-weed
### *Epilobium ciliatum* Raf. var. *glandulosum* (Lehm.) Dorn

The common willow-weed has clusters of tiny (less than 1/4 inch), bell-shaped flowers with four deeply notched petals. It blooms from July to mid-August along mountain streams and in other moist situations. Its stems and foliage feel sticky hence the name *glandulosum* (a "gland," botanically implies a secreting cell with sticky secretions). Note the long tubular "stem" that houses an ovary; this matures into a pod-like seed capsule. The plant is found throughout the West, north to Alaska, in all of Canada, and in most of our northern states.

### Common evening-primrose
### *Oenothera villosa* Thunb. var. *strigosa* (Rydb.) Dorn

The common (or hairy) evening-primrose is found throughout the United States and Canada, save in a few southern states. Several varieties are recognized; ours is a western plant found mostly in the Rocky Mountains (the species name, *villosa,* and the variety name, *strigosa,* both imply that the plant is covered with fine hairs) growing at least as high as the montane zone. Like the rock-rose shown below, this plant has a showy flower whose blooms last but a day. It is usually found in open meadows where it is easily identified by its alternate lanceolate leaves, four large yellow petals and reflexed (bent downward) sepals.

### Rock-rose
### *Oenothera cespitosa* Nutt.
### var. *cespitosa*

The rock-rose, known by many other local names, is a wide-ranging western plant. It flowers late in the summer and is often found high in our mountains growing on exposed, dry, sandy slopes. Oenotheras bloom at night when moth-pollinators are active, and by the next afternoon the flowers have wilted—today's and yesterday's flowers are present in the illustration below. As you hike, you had best photograph this showy flower on your way up, as it will be past prime on the descent! The plant's specific epithet is properly spelled *caespitosa* (the term means "tufted"). Our spelling, *cespitosa,* is correct, however, as Thomas Nuttall spelled the word that way in describing it; according to the rules of botanical nomenclature the first published name establishes the correct orthography for a plant.

# Peony Family (Paeoniaceae)

The peony family is a small one, consisting of only one genus and 33 species. Typically white-petaled, most are perennial shrubs or small trees whose alternate leaves are divided into three lobes, each lobe, in turn, divides into three or more smaller lobes. The flowers are usually large, radially symmetrical, with five sepals, five petals (or occasionally ten), and many stamens. Five large seed capsules form while the plant is still flowering, each contains many seeds. The family's chief commercial value is for its cultivars—well known ornamental garden varieties with showy blossoms. Peonies were named by Theophrastus (372-c.287 B.C.), Aristotle's pupil and the author of an important work on botany. The name honors Apollo who, in his role as Paean, physician to the gods, used the plant medicinally. Certain species of peony are still used in folk medicine (*e.g.*, the European alpine plant *Paeonia officianalis* and an Asian tree, *Paeonia suffruticosa*), although they seem to have no proven therapeutic worth.

Only two peonies are native to North America. The western peony, *Paeonia brownii* shown on the following page, grows in all of the northwestern states and south to California, Nevada and Utah. The similar California peony, *Paeonia californica*, is found only in that state.

**Western peony**
*Paeonia brownii* Douglas ex Hook.

One might not relate the western peony's flowers to those of the popular garden plant, nevertheless, they are close cousins. Our plants grow as high as the subalpine zone and are often seen along hiking trails, in canyon bottoms and on nearby sagebrush slopes, blooming in mid- to late spring. The large flowers nod and may be hard to see at first glance, although the plant's light green, deeply incised leaves stand out conspicuously against the surrounding sagebrush. The flower is so unusual that it is easily identified. Strangely, the wild peony is not mentioned in Coulter's compendious *Manual of Rocky Mountain Botany* (1885), although David Douglas had collected the plant in the mountains of today's Oregon in 1826. Douglas suggested that it be named for Robert Brown (1773-1858) one of England's most prominent botanists. William Jackson Hooker described it several years later in his *Flora Boreali-Americana* (1829) and followed Douglas's suggestion in naming the plant.

## Phlox Family (Polemoniaceae)

The phlox family consists of twenty genera and 360 species. Most are found in North America although a few are native to temperate parts of South America and Eurasia. Many species in the family have been cultivated as garden ornamentals: phlox, Jacob's ladder, gilias, and others that represent the family's only economic importance. Flowers in this family are usually clustered and sometimes form a head in which the upper flowers are the first to bloom (botanically, a "cyme"). Five sepals and five petals unite at the base to form a flower tube. At the point that the petals become separate they flare outward , and the flowers then are variously referred to as being trumpet-, funnel-, or saucer-shaped (the latter are "salverform"). Fourteen genera of Polemoniaceae occur in the Northwest. At least half of them are represented in Idaho. The plants in some of the genera are so small that they would easily escape notice unless one is looking for them. The word "Polemoniaceae" is derived from "polemonium" the name of a European alpine wildflower, *Polemonium caeruleum* L., commonly known as Jacob's ladder or Greek valerian, a plant that has been cultivated as an ornamental for centuries. The origin of the word "polemonium," in turn, is uncertain; several derivations have been suggested. It may be that  the plant was named for Polemon, a second century B.C. Greek philosopher and one of of Aristotle's successors as head of the Lyceum in Athens.

### Narrow-leaf collomia
### *Collomia linearis* Nutt.

The narrow-leaf collomia is widely distributed, occurring in all Canadian provinces and in all but our southern states. Its five-petaled flowers are about a quarter of an inch in diameter, with a long flower tube. The name *linearis* describes the plant's narrow leaves; *collomia*, from the Greek, means "glue," because the seeds become mucilaginous when wet—a property that helps to identify plants in this family. The narrow-leaf collomia is so common in early spring that anyone hiking in our mountains will see it. Lewis and Clark were first to collect this plant (April 17th, 1806), when portaging around the falls of the Columbia at today's The Dalles, Oregon, on their homeward journey. Frederick Pursh, who described the expedition's plants, did not recognize their specimen as a new species so the explorers received no credit for finding it; it remained for Thomas Nuttall to find it again. A tiny-flowered, similar species, the diffuse collomia (*Collomia tenella* A. Gray, not shown) is another common collomia that grows at high elevations.

### Brewer's navarretia
### *Navarretia breweri* (A. Gray) Greene

Brewer's navarretia's yellow flowers measure no more than 1/8 inch across. Typically, several flowers grow at the end of the stems, surrounded by needle-shaped leaves (navarretias are also known as "pin-cushion plants"). The appearance is unique, making it easy to identify. The long flower tube and five-petaled flowers help place it in the phlox family. Brewer's navarretia grows in the Rocky Mountains (save New Mexico) and west to the three Pacific states. The genus was named for Francisco Fernandez Navarrete (d. 1689), a Spanish missionary, physician, and botanist. William Henry Brewer (1828-1910), for whom the species was named, was an associate of mineralogist Josiah Dwight Whitney (1819-1896; he of Mt. Whitney) while surveying California (1860-1864) and subsequently became professor of agriculture at Yale from 1864 to 1903.

### Slender phlox
### *Microsteris gracilis* (Hook.) Greene
### var. *humilior* (Hook.) Cronquist

The slender phlox is a variable plant that appears in the spring. Sometimes—like the collomia (above)—in large numbers. Its flowers may be pink or white; pink is most common. The flowers are borne in pairs, although they do not always bloom at the same time. Typically its petals are notched at the end. Elliptical, opposed leaves become narrower and more pointed toward the top of the stem. The plant is only about two inches high, so single plants are easily missed. Its varietal name *humilior* means "low-growing" or "dwarf." It occurs throughout the west as far north as Alaska. The name *Microsteris* was derived from the Greek *mikros* (small) and *sterizo* (to support, or prop up) evidently having to do with the plant's small size.

### Spreading phlox
### *Phlox diffusa* Benth.
### var. *longistylis* (Wherry) M. E. Peck

The word *phlox* ("flame" in ancient Greek) was the name of a now unknown plant. Later, it was given to our flowers. Despite their worldwide popularity as ornamentals, all phlox cultivars seem to have been derived from North American plants. About eighteen species grow in the Northwest; this one, *Phlox diffusa*, is common in our mountains, growing in clumps of narrow gray-green leaves surmounted by a profusion of usually white flowers, although pink and lavender forms are common. Spreading phlox dots rocky slopes from early April at mid-elevations, well into the summer at timberline and higher. The species occurs in all of our western states and provinces. A rather similar species, *Phlox hoodii* Richardson, is common at lower altitudes.

### Longleaf phlox
### *Phlox longifolia* Nutt.

The longleaf phlox grows at all elevations, blooming from late in the spring well into the summer; as always, depending on the altitude. The plant is taller and characterized by narrower petals, longer leaves and less tightly clustered flowers than those of the spreading phlox shown above; the two plants have a similar distribution. Nathaniel Wyeth (he of the wyethias) collected the original specimens in 1833 in Idaho or Montana, and his friend Thomas Nuttall described the species the following year.

### Showy phlox
### *Phlox speciosa* Pursh

The showy phlox grows at lower elevations than do those shown above. It often grows in the company of sagebrush in the foothills and lower mountain ranges. It is more common in the northern half of Idaho. Lewis and Clark collected the plant on May 7, 1806, while in what today is Nez Perce County on their return journey. Showy phlox is found from British Columbia south to California's Sierra Nevada, into Nevada and west to Montana. The plant is easily identified, for this is the only phlox in our area with prominently notched petals. An attractive plant, the showy phlox makes a good garden ornamental.

### Western jacob's-ladder
### *Polemonium occidentale* Greene

The western Jacob's-ladder is a moist-meadow and streamside plant that grows to be a foot or more high. It is so closely related to an uncommon European alpine, *Polemonium caeruleum* that some botanists believe that ours is a variety of that plant and classify it as such. Our plants grow as high as the subalpine zone. Furry stems are topped with one or more small, five-petaled bright blue flowers. Prominent yellow anthers on long filaments add to the flower's attractive appearance. The name Jacob's-ladder reflects the plant's feathery compound leaves, common to the genus. These give off a pronounced skunk-like odor when crushed; the smell may be the first indication that polemoniums are growing nearby. The plants grow in all of the Rocky Mountain states save New Mexico and Arizona, north to Canada's Yukon Territory. A disjunct population is found in northern Minnesota.

### Showy polemonium
### *Polemonium pulcherrimum* Hook.

Lewis and Clark collected a species of polemonium on the Lolo trail on June 27, 1806. Originally it was believed to be *Polemonium occidentale* (shown above). It seems more likely, however, that it was the showy polemonium, a common species along their trail on that date. While the plant shown here—photographed on a shady slope near Lolo Pass—has pale blue flowers, those growing in the open are often bright blue. The species name, *pulcherrimum*, means "most beautiful." Several varieties are recognized. Ours, var. *pulcherrimum*, grows east to Montana, Wyoming and Utah, and west to the Pacific coastal states and provinces, and north to Alaska.

### Sticky polemonium
### *Polemonium viscosum* Nutt.

The sticky polemonium (or Jacob's ladder) grows in Washington, Oregon, Idaho, and Alberta, then south to Arizona and New Mexico. It is an attractive, low-growing plant with deep blue flowers and pinnate leaves populated with small, tightly ranked leaflets. When crushed, this plant's leaves give off a strong skunk-like odor—"skunk polemonium" is another common name. The plants grow in separate clumps and are found quite high—we have seen small specimens growing well above treeline.

**Scarlet gilia**
***Ipomopsis aggregata***
**(Pursh) V. Grant**

The scarlet gilia (formerly classified as *Gilia aggregata*) blooms in late spring, peaks in early summer, and lingers on into late summer according to the altitude. One cannot hike our trails without encountering its trumpet-shaped, bright red flowers. The flowers and foliage have an acrid odor when crushed, so "skunkflower" is another name for the plant, although the odor really is not skunk-like. The scarlet gilia is one of the few flowers (with Indian paintbrushes) that add dots of bright red to a landscape dominated by greens and browns. The name *Gilia* honors an Italian naturalist and clergyman, Filippo Luigi Gil (1756-1821), the Director of the Vatican observatory. The species name "*aggregata*" refers to the loose flower clusters. The present generic name, *Ipomopsis* means "morning glory-like." Lewis and Clark collected the scarlet gilia—a plant hitherto unknown to science—while on the Lolo trail in northern Idaho during their return trip (June 26, 1806). Although the explorers waited until then to gather their specimen, they would surely have have seen it in Idaho's mountains during their outbound journey in the summer of 1805. A common name "scarlet skyrocket" has been suggested for this plant.

### Ball-head gilia
### *Ipomopsis congesta*
### (Hook.) V. Grant

Here is another gilia that has been reclassified as an *Ipomopsis*. The species name, *congesta*, reflects the plant's round flower head, with its many tiny phlox-like flowers. It grows high in the mountains on dry sandy slopes, blooming in mid-summer. The leaves are silvery-green, usually with three linear leaflets, arising from a central branched woody stem. Nine varieties of this plant are recognized, classified mostly by the shape of the leaves; ours is var. *viridis* (Cronquist) Reveal. The plants, as one variety or another, are found in most states west of the Mississippi.

### Nuttall's leptosiphon
### *Leptosiphon nuttallii*
### (A. Gray) J. M. Porter
### & L. A. Johnson

This attractive plant (originally classified as *Linanthastrum* and more recently as *Linanthus*) is a common, summer-blooming wildflower that grows as high as treeline. Typically, it forms a discrete clump. Its linear, alternate leaves are so close together that they appear to form separate rosettes on the plants' woody stems. White, yellow-eyed flowers are five-petaled; each has five prominent anthers. At times there are so many flowers as to completely cover the plants. These give off a faint, sweet odor. Thomas Nuttall found the species, then new to science, near Fort Hall in 1834. The name *Leptosiphon* is a recently restored old classification derived from the Greek; it means "slender tube" for the narrow flower tube.

## Buckwheat Family (Polygonaceae)

The name, Polygonaceae, is derived from two Greek words; *poly* meaning "many" and *goni* for "joint", a reference to species that have swollen stem-nodes or joints.* The family is made up of fifty-two genera and approximately 1,105 species. Typically, members have smooth-bordered, unlobed leaves and flowerheads made up of tight clusters of small flowers. Varying numbers of sepals (three to six) substitute for petals. In some species an accessory structure known as an "ocrea" forms a sheath around the main stems at the node where the leaves join it. A few Polygonaceae are commercially important as ornamentals and as food plants, including buckwheat (*Polygonum esculenta*), sorrel (several *Rumex* species) and rhubarb (*Rheum rhaponticum*). The latter—in common with other members of the family—contains oxalic acid responsible for the plant's acidic juice. Other species of rhubarb (e.g., *Rheum officinale*) were used in the past as purgatives, and a few species have found a place in ornamental gardens.

———

*This derivation is debated. Some believe that the *gon-* stem refers to "seeds" rather than "joints." Thus Polygonaceae would imply "many seeds."

**Sulphurflower wild buckwheat**
*Eriogonum umbellatum* **Torr.**
**var.** *ellipticum* **(Nutt.) Reveal**

The sulphurflower wild buckwheat is sometimes known as the "umbrella buckwheat," possibly a better name, for it reflects the species name *umbellatum* (Latin for "umbrella") referring to the flowerheads and their stems, reminiscent of the umbels that characterize the parsley family (Apiaceae). This species is found from the Rocky Mountain states, west to the Pacific Coast and north to British Columbia. At last count some forty varieties were recognized. The variety shown here is localized to portions of Washington, Oregon and Idaho and has a highly branched umbellate inflorescence. Another variety, with cream-colored flowers and a simple umbel, var. *dichrocephalum* Gandoger, is also common in our area.

*Eriogonum* is by far the largest genus of Polygonaceae in our mountains. The genus is made up mostly of western North American plants—more are shown on the following page. The number of species in the genus is outnumbered only by the number of penstemons (*Penstemon* spp.) and of the milk vetches (*Astragalus* spp.). As with those plants, identification of wild buckwheats is often difficult, made more so by hybridization, and variations in form and color.

**Purple cushion wild buckwheat**
*Eriogonum ovalifolium* **Nutt.**
**var.** *purpureum* **(Nutt.) Durand**

The purple cushion wild buckwheat occurs in all western mountain states and provinces. It is characterized by small, oval, gray-green leaves, a tightly formed flowerhead and creamy white flowers that develop purple coloration as they mature.

**Dwarf cushion wild buckwheat**
*Eriogonum ovalifolium* **Nutt.**
**var.** *depressum* **Blank.**

The dwarf cushion wild buckwheat is native to the northern Rocky Mountains, growing at subalpine to alpine elevations. When mature, its flowers are often bright red. The cushion buckwheats shown on this page are two of eleven varieties of *Eriogonum ovalifolium.*

**Hitchcock's wild buckwheat**
*Eriogonum capistratum* **Reveal**
**var.** *capistratum*

Hitchcock's wild buckwheat is an eye-catching, matted plant made up of tightly clustered tiny gray leaves and two-tone yellow and red flowers. While this variety occurs in the foothills and lower mountains of central Idaho, an alpine variety, var. *muhlickii,* is found in the high mountains of western Montana.

**Piper's wild buckwheat**
*Eriogonum flavum* **Nutt.**
**var.** *piperi* **(Greene) M. E. Jones**

Many eriogonums have yellow flowers, none are brighter than those of this plant. Its narrow lanceolate leaves are usually smooth on top and hairy beneath. The plants prefer rocky ground at high altitudes. It is found in the mountains of our Northwest and as far north as Alaska.

**Parsnip-flower wild buckwheat**
*Eriogonum heracleoides* **Nutt.**

This eriogonum grows in the northern Rocky Mountains and west to mountains in Oregon and California. In Idaho it is a montane plant, often the dominant valley wildflower in the dry heat of early summer. A whorl of bracts, mid-stem below the creamy-white flowerhead, identifies the plant.

**Hairy Shasta wild buckwheat**
*Eriogonum pyrolifolium* **Hook.**
**var.** *coryphaeum* **Torr. & A. Gray**

A high altitude plant, the alpine wild buckwheat grows near treeline, where it blooms soon after snow-melt. Identify it by its smooth, bright green basal leaves and white flowerheads. It is native to the high mountains of all four states of the Northwest.

# Polygonaceae

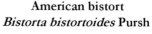

## American bistort
### *Bistorta bistortoides* Pursh

The American bistort grows in mountain meadows throughout the West. The name is an old one, derived from the Latin *bis* (twice) and *torta* (twisted) and applied to a similar Eurasian plant. It refers to the plants' bulky twisted roots. These store the food required for rapid growth during a short growing season. The American bistort blooms from June well into August. Small white flowers form well delineated clusters at the top of spindly stems. Both the roots and the young leaves of the bistort are edible and were used as food by Native Americans; the flowers and foliage are grazed by deer, and bears dig up the roots. Lewis and Clark were the first to collect this plant, on the Wieppe Prairie in north central Idaho (June 12, 1806) on their return journey. Recent genetic studies suggest that this plant deserves to be classified as its own genus, or in the same genus as the Eurasian bistort, rather than as a species of *Polygonum* as the plant was formerly classified.

The larger illustration above shows white American bistort, interspersed with bright orange Indian paintbrush, growing above treeline at the foot of Old Hyndman Peak, in central Idaho's Pioneer Range.

## Poke knotweed
### *Polygonum phytolaccifolium* Meisn. ex Small

The poke knotweed, variously known also as the alpine knotweed, pokeweed, or fleeceflower, bears some slight resemblance to the common pokeweed (*Phytolacca americana* in the family Phytolaccaceae), and the species name, *phytolaccifolium*, implies that its leaves resemble pokeweed leaves.* The poke knotweed is a common subalpine plant found in moist situations where it blooms from mid-summer on. Given its distinctive appearance, it is unlikely to be confused with any other Polygonaceae. While it is without food value for humans, animals graze freely on the plant.

---

*The etymology of the *lacc-* stem is interesting. It is derived from a Hindustani word, *lakh*, for an insect that secretes a bright red, sticky material used as a pigment—whence the artist's color "crimson lake." The same material, when decolorized and dried is know as "shell lac"—whence "shellac."

### Mountain sheep sorrel
### *Rumex paucifolius* Nutt.

The mountain sorrel's clustered flowers turn conspicuously red as they fruit so the plants form red patches in mountain meadows where they grow. The name, *paucifolius*, means "few-leaved," pertaining only to the flower-bearing stems, for the plants have many lance-shaped basal leaves. *Rumex* is the Latin word for "sorrel." The genus also includes the edible sorrel, *Rumex acetosa*, whose acidic taste is derived from the oxalic acid common to the leaves of all species of *Rumex*. The plants grow in most of our western states. They are unrelated to wood sorrels (*Oxalidaceae*, *Oxalis* spp.) whose foliage also contains oxalic acid.

### Willow dock
### *Rumex salicifolius* Weinm.
### var. *triangulivalvis*
### (Danser) J.C. Hickman

Willow dock grows in most of the United States. Six (of seven) varieties are found in the Northwest. The variety shown here is restricted to high elevations in the northern Rocky Mountains. The name, *salicifolius*, means "willow-like leaves." At first glance, it is not an especially attractive plant, although the flowers and the fruit ("achenes," shown here on the right) are rather striking. Willow dock is considered a weed in much of its range, but our plant grows too high to have a weedy impact on anything. The varietal name, *triangulivalvis* refers to the form of the plant's fruit.

# Purslane Family (Portulacaceae)

The purslane family, Portulacaceae (28 genera, 440 species), gets its name from an Old World potherb, *Portulaca oleracea*. Pliny, in his Natural History (1st century A.D.), named the plant *porcil-aka*, a word with no known meaning that, in time, became portulaca. Then, because it sounded like "porcelain," the flower's common name in England became "purslane," a word in use since the fourteenth century. The common purslane, the only European member of the family, is still grown there as a potherb. Introduced to America, it has spread throughout the United States and is now a troublesome, fleshy-leaved, garden weed (although Harrington, in *Edible Native Plants of the Rocky Mountains*, extols the edible virtues of this easily identifiable plant). Most members of the purslane family are found in the temperate zones of the Americas and are well represented in our Northwest Distinguishing family features include: large roots (used by Indians as food); fleshy leaves (edible in some species); showy flowers (some are cultivated as ornamental plants, the family's only commercial importance); four to many petals; and, in most, two sepals (a distinguishing feature).

**Common bitter-root  (above, above right)**
*Lewisia rediviva* **Pursh**

Frederick Pursh recognized this plant as a new genus, naming it for Meriwether Lewis who obtained it at "Traveler's Rest" near today's Missoula, Montana (July 1, 1806). Pursh named the species *rediviva,* meaning "return to life," because one of Lewis's specimens bloomed when planted after the expedition's return. The bitter-root's striking, many-petaled flowers appear on gravelly ground in late spring. In Blaine and Camas counties (and south to Nevada) the flowers are white; farther north they are varying shades of pink. Bitter-root grows in British Columbia and Alberta, south to Colorado and northern Arizona. Indians prized the roots, but white-men found them unpalatable, explaining the plant's common name.

**Alpine bitter-root (below, below left)**
*Lewisia pygmaea* **(A. Gray) B. L. Robins**

The pink-flowered alpine, or pygmy bitter-root (var. *pygmaea*) grows on bare ground, from the subalpine zone to well above tree-line. The plants are tiny—those pictured below were less than 1/4" in diameter, and no part extends more than an inch above ground level. It is difficult to see how the plant survives, subjected to harsh winds and freezing temperatures, but microclimate is everything. There is little wind at ground level, and rocky tundra, warmed by the sun, radiates warmth. So long as the plant hugs the ground, it survives. The white form on the left is occasionally seen in Idaho. It appears to be var. *nevadensis* (A. Gray) B. L. Robins. The pygmy bitter-root grows in all of the Rocky Mountain states.

**Siberian springbeauty**
*Claytonia sibirica* L.

**Miner's lettuce**
*Claytonia perfoliata*
Donn ex. Willd.

**Streambank springbeauty**
*Claytonia parviflora*
Dougl. ex Hook.

## Springbeauties and Candyflowers

Species of *Montia* (candyflowers) and *Claytonia* (springbeauties) are so closely related that most have been cross-classified between the two genera over the years. Consensus now favors the classification used here. The top four plants were collected by Meriwether Lewis in the spring of 1806, on the Columbia and Clearwater rivers. The name Claytonia honors Virginia botanist John Clayton (1694-1773) who collected the eastern springbeauty *Claytonia virginica*.

**Siberian springbeauties** are found in all of the Pacific coastal states, north to Alaska and inland to Idaho and Montana. A streamside plant, it is characterized by broad leaves and loose clusters of dainty white flowers.

**Miner's-lettuce** grows in all of the western states, north to Alaska. It is an unusual springbeauty because its stems pierce two opposing conjoined leaves. The plant is best known for its use as a salad green in the early days of the West, hence its common name.

**Streambank springbeauty** is a reclusive plant found in the Rocky Mountain and Pacific coastal states, favoring moist woods and quiet streambanks. It is the least common of the plants on this page.

**Lanceleaf springbeauty** bears white-petaled flowers, with pink veins and anthers. Some years, for reasons that are obscure, many of the flowers appear pink, as in our illustration. The plant is common throughout the West, blooming soon after snowmelt on open ground. Lanceolate leaves give the plant its species name.

**Heart-leaf springbeauty** prefers deeply shaded, moist forests. Its name, *cordifolia*, describes the plant's wide, heart-shaped leaves. It is native to the northern Rocky Mountain and Pacific coastal states.

**Chamisso's candyflower** is usually classified as a species of *Montia* (candyflowers) rather than as a *Claytonia* (springbeauties). It is named for the German botanist who discovered the plant (see p. 144). While all springbeauties prefer moist, or recently moist, soil, this plant grows in the water of spring puddles and freshets.

**Lanceleaf springbeauty**
*Claytonia lanceolata* Pall. ex Pursh

**Heartleaf springbeauty**
*Claytonia cordifolia* S. Watson

**Chamisso's candyflower**
*Montia chamissoi*
(Ledeb. ex Spreng.) Greene

## Primrose Family (Primulaceae)

The primrose family's common name was derived from the term "prime rose" applied to certain flowers—daisies, primroses, and others—that bloom early in the spring. The family consists of 18 genera, and 955 species. Its members typically have radially symmetrical flowers whose five (occasionally four) petals may join for part or all of their length into a tube. Most are perennial, herbaceous (non-woody) and native to the north temperate zone. Subalpine and alpine Primulaceae are found in all of the mountain ranges of the northern hemisphere. Many primulas are grown as ornamental cultivars (primroses, shooting stars, cyclamens, etc.); otherwise the family has little commercial importance.

### Jeffrey's shooting star
### *Dodecatheon jeffreyi* Van Houtte

Jeffrey's, or mountain shooting stars, grow on the banks of mountain lakes and in mucky meadows moist from melting snow. They bloom as high as treeline, sometimes in profuse numbers, from late spring well into summer, according to elevation. The flowers have five (occasionally four) swept back, white-based, pink petals with a yellow collar at the base. Purple-brown anthers join to form a point from which the filament protrudes. Although it may take a hand lens to see it, the stigma at the end of the filament is about twice the width of the filament, a distinguishing feature for the species. The name *Dodecatheon* comes from the Greek and means "twelve gods"; the significance of the name is obscure. Jeffrey's shooting star grows from California to Alaska and in the northwestern states. Although we have retained the classification *Dodecatheon* for shooting stars, recent studies have shown that they actually belong to genus *Primula*, and have been (as of 2007) so classified). They differ from other primroses only in their mode of pollination.

### Many-flowered shooting star
### *Dodecatheon pulchellum*
### (Raf.) Merr.

The many-flowered (or dark-throat) shooting star is another *Dodecatheon* often encountered in Idaho's mountains. While both this species and Jeffrey's shooting star, shown on the previous page, are western plants, *Dodecatheon pulchellum* is more widely distributed; it is found in most states and provinces west of the Mississippi River. A squiggly purple ring at the base of the petals is a distinguishing characteristic, as is the size of the stigma which—unlike that of Jeffrey's shooting star—is the same diameter as the filament. Shooting stars typically have a rosette of basal leaves, the shape of the leaves varies with the species. The stem is naked, topped with one to several flowers. Botanists recognize several varieties of this species, differentiated chiefly by the color of the anthers. The plant in the illustration, with pale yellow anthers is var. *cusickii* (Greene) Reveal. The term *pulchellum*, from the Latin, means "beautiful."

### Rocky Mountain androsace
### *Androsace montana* A. Gray

Until recently this plant, also known as a "dwarf primrose," was classified as *Douglasia montana*. On the basis of recent studies, however, it is now classified as an androsace (andros-a-KEY). The Rocky Mountain androsace is a low, mat-forming, vibrant pink-flowered plant. The flowers have a small, ringed, central "eye," common to primroses in general. It is a true alpine plant, found only in the mountains of Idaho, Wyoming, Montana, and rarely in Alberta. Other species of *Androsace* occur everywhere in North America, to the arctic and Greenland, excepting in a few southern and eastern seaboard states.

**Cusick's primrose**
***Primula cusickiana***
**(A. Gray) A. Gray**

Cusick's primrose is an early spring-blooming, subalpine plant whose yellow-eyed flowers range from pale to deep purple. It is found only in the Wallowa Mountains of north-eastern Oregon and in central Idaho where it blooms, after snowmelt, on rough, seemingly unpromising ground. The species is named for William Cusick (1842-1922), a rancher, teacher and botanist who collected plants in the Northwest. Attempts to cultivate this elegant little flower have not been successful.

Parry's (or brook) primrose, *Primula parryi* A. Gray (not shown), is another subalpine plant in the same genus. It also grows in Idaho and in the other Rocky Mountain states, although we have not encountered it. The plant is considerably larger than Cusick's primrose—its leaves may be ten inches or more in length. The flowers are reddish-purple with yellow eyes. The plant prefers moist surroundings.

# Buttercup Family (Ranunculaceae)

The buttercup family is a moderately large one, made up of 58 genera and nearly 2,505 species. Because of the flowers' simple configurations and frequent lack of petals, the family is considered to be one of the more primitive of the dicotyledons. While most members are herbaceous (non-woody) plants, a few are woody shrubs or vines. The family favors the north temperate zone and is very well represented in our Northwest. Although it's a surprisingly diverse family, one whose members take many forms, there are common characteristics: flower parts are free and not joined; many members have petal-like sepals and true petals are often lacking; the leaves are usually compound and three-parted, and the plants favor moist environments.

Most of the Ranunculaceae produce poisonous alkaloids. Some of these are therapeutically active, although seldom used today, having been supplanted by safer and more effective medications. Aside from the negative impact that ingesting certain of the Ranunculaceae, (*Delphinium* spp. especially) has on cattle and sheep, many members of the family have showy blooms and have found a place in ornamental gardens; e.g., species of *Aconitum* (monkshood), *Aquilegia* (columbine), *Clematis*, *Delphinium* (larkspurs), *Ranunculus*, etc.; these represent the family's chief economic importance. The generic name *Ranunculus* (from which the family name is derived) is a diminutive form of the Latin *rana*, the word for "frog"; i.e., something that grows in wet places.

**Red baneberry (above, above left)**
***Actaea rubra* (Ait.) Willd.**

The baneberry grows in all of the northern states and Canadian provinces, mostly on the banks of shaded streams. Short-lived white flowers form tight clusters. The shrub's red (occasionally white) berries are poisonous. Some plant poisons when used medicinally do have therapeutic benefit. A tincture derived from the European baneberry, *Actaea spicata*, has been used as a folk medicine to treat pulmonary problems. The name *Actaea* is from a Greek word for the elderberry; the plant's leaflets apparently resemble the leaves of a European elder. The name *rubra* means "red" for the berries. The common name is derived from the Old English word "bane," a word that means "poison."

**Western monkshood**
***Aconitum columbianum* Nutt. (left)**

This plant is the only species of monkshood found in the Northwest. It flowers in midsummer in wet meadows, seep-springs, and along stream banks at mid- to high elevations. Deep purple flowers are spaced along the top of a tall stem. The "hood" is a petal-like sepal that encloses two small petals. All parts of the plants are poisonous. Criminals were executed and wolves were poisoned with a distillate from *Aconitum lycoctonum*, the European wolf's-bane. The same plant was also supposedly a component of witches' brews. Although the monkshood's flowers, like those of the related larkspur, are almost always purple, occasionally albino forms turn up, as shown in the inset. The plant is found in British Columbia, the Rocky Mountain states, then west to the Pacific coast, and east to South Dakota and Iowa.

### American pasqueflower
### *Anemone patens* L.
### var. *multifida* Pritz.

Our pasqueflower is a lovely plant with large flowers and sepals that range in color from light blue to deep purple. Deeply incised leaves are characteristic and distinguish this plant from the similar western pasqueflower, *Anemone occidentalis*, whose leaves are less dissected; it too grows in Idaho. The American pasqueflower is found in all of the Rocky Mountain states, east to the Great Lakes and north to Alaska. The name "pasqueflower" has long been used for a European anemone. John Gerard (1545-1612) in his *Herbal* of 1597 wrote, "They flower for the most part about Easter, which hath mooved me to name it Pasque flower, or Easter flower."

### Cliff anemone
### *Anemone multifida* Poir.

The cliff anemone grows on moist ground, from mid-elevations to alpine tundra. The name, *multifida*, means "much divided" referring to its deeply divided leaves. The flowers are "apetalous," i.e, the "petals"—usually five or six—are actually petal-like sepals. These vary greatly in color, from off-white, through ochroleucous (pale yellow) to deep red, bluish, or even purple. The plant grows in the West and all across the northern part of the continent. Given the amount of variation, it is not surprising to learn that a half dozen varieties are recognized. The rosette of leaves (bracts) on the stem below the flower is a distinguishing feature of anemones in general.

### Small-flowered anemone
### *Anemone parviflora* Michx.

The small-flowered, or northern anemone is usually found growing close to water, in moist meadows and on streambanks, often at subalpine elevations. Each plant bears a single flower made up of petaloid sepals. In the center many yellow stamens surround a spherical head made up of green achenes. This anemone may be confused with other white-blossomed Ranunculaceae, especially the marsh marigold, *Caltha leptosepala* (shown below) and the globeflower, *Trollius laxus* (page 179). Anemone from the Greek is said to mean "daughter of the wind," explaining why anemones are also known as "windflowers." Another common name, "thimble-weed," reflects the appearance of the fruiting head.

### Piper's anemone
### *Anemone piperi* Britton ex Rydb.

Piper's anemone is common in the mountains of north-central Idaho, in the adjacent corners of Washington and Oregon, and in western Montana. It is characterized by three compound leaves below a single, delicate white flower. It prefers the moist ground of shaded forests. Meriwether Lewis collected this—then unnamed—anemone near the Clearwater River on June 15, 1806. Frederick Pursh who classified the expedition's material dropped the ball; apparently he concluded that Lewis's specimen was the same plant as an eastern anemone, and did not include it with other expedition specimens in his *Flora* of 1813.

### White marsh marigold
### *Caltha leptosepala* DC.

The marsh marigold is an early blooming subalpine to alpine plant often found in profuse numbers in wet mountain meadows and on the banks of the seasonal ponds that form as snow melts. Its deep green leaves grow into an elongated heart shape, followed by the appearance of one to several stems, each bearing a showy white flower with a bright yellow center. Its "petals" are petaliform sepals that are sometimes tinged with blue. *Caltha* is a Latin word used for a yellow marigold; *leptosepala*, means "slender sepals." The plant grows in all of the far western states, north to Alaska.

### Sitka columbine
### *Aquilegia formosa* Fisch. ex DC.

The Sitka (also red, or crimson) columbine is a handsome flower. Tall, with distinctive three-parted leaves, its sepals vary in color from pale orange to bright red, depending on growth conditions. These are set off by five, red-based, yellow petals and many long yellow anthers. The plants flower from late spring through midsummer, as high as treeline. Look for it in open forests, along streams, and on high rocky slopes soon after the snow pack has melted.

The scientific name *Aquilegia* was derived from the Latin word *acquila* meaning "eagle," because the flower's five spurs were thought to resemble an eagle's claws. The species name, *formosa*, also from the Latin, means "beautiful." Paradoxically—given the derivation of the generic name—"columbine" means "dove-like" because the spurs in some species are said to be shaped like the head and neck of a dove. *Aquilegia coerulea* E. James, the lovely blue Colorado state flower, grows in the southeastern corner of Idaho, although we have not encountered it.

### Yellow columbine
### *Aquilegia flavescens* S. Watson

The yellow columbine is another montane to alpine species that grows in Idaho's mountains, although it is less common than the Sitka columbine. It is easily identified by its soft yellow sepals ranging at times to a pinkish color. It is closely related to *Aquilegia formosa* and the two species may form hybrids. All gradations of color between the vivid red and yellow of the former plant, and the overall soft yellow of this one are seen from time to time.

### Western virgin's bower
### *Clematis occidentalis* (Hornem.) *DC.*
### *var. grosseserrata* (Rydb.) **J. S. Pringle**

The western virgin's bower is a woody climbing vine of the mountain west. The flowers are apetalous and its purple sepals stand out in the shade of the montane forests that the plant prefers. Three-parted leaves with toothed, heart-shaped leaflets are a clue that it is in the buttercup family. A similar plant that differs in the shape of its leaves, *Clematis columbiana (Nutt.)* Torr. & Gray, is found in the south-eastern part of Idaho. The Greek word *klematis* referred originally to a periwinkle (*Vinca* sp.) and later was applied to this genus.

### Vase-flower, *Clematis hirsutissima* **Pursh**

This plant, known also as the "sugar-bowl," "leather-flower" and "hairy (*hirsutissimma*) clematis," could not be mistaken for any other. Four purple sepals are joined for much of their length to form a furry "vase" that gives the flower one of its common names. It is a herbaceous (non-woody) soft-stemmed, perennial plant, with flowers borne on a single stem that arises from a profusion of leaves that divide into narrow leaflets. Vase-flowers prefer moist meadows, blooming in mid spring to early summer. The plant was unknown to science until Lewis and Clark collected it in on May 27, 1806, near their encampment on the Clearwater River near today's Kamiah, Idaho. It grows in all of the Rocky Mountain states as well as in the four northwestern states.

### Western clematis, *Clematis ligusticifolia* **Nutt.**

The western clematis (or western virgin's bower) is native to most of the western states and Canadian provinces, south to northern Mexico. The plants prefer dry, open ground where they form aggressive, rapidly spreading vines that cover neighboring trees, shrubs and fences. They form masses of white blossoms, followed by densely hairy fruiting bodies (seen also in other members of the genus). In this plant the fruiting bodies often coalesce to cover the plant. The western clematis is sometimes used as an ornamental, but it tends to spread further and faster than one might wish. The species name *ligusticifolia* apparently refers to a perceived similarity between this plant's leaves and those of a species of *Ligusticum* in the parsley family (Apiaceae).

### Upland larkspur
### *Delphinium nuttallianum* Pritz. (above)

The upland larkspur grows as high as treeline in all the Rocky Mountain states. It is often found on over-grazed land. Cattlemen hate the plant for it poisons livestock—a good example of the maxim "my wildflower, your weed." The plants are usually only six to ten inches high, and flower early in the spring on dry ground, often surrounded by sagebrush. Delphinium flowers are made up of five outer sepals that enclose much smaller petals. The upper sepal forms the distinctive spur. This plant's flower color varies from deep blue or purple, through an attractive soft blue-gray (upper right), to white. Regardless of the flower color, some blue marking is always retained on the upper petals.

### Slim larkspur
### *Delphinium depauperatum* Nutt. (left)

Several tall larkspurs grow in our mountains; the slim larkspur is one of the more common ones (the species name, *depauperatum* means "impoverished," although it doesn't seem to fit the plant). It may grow as a solitary plant, or as a cluster, in meadows and in the partial shade of open woods. Telling the various *Delphinium* species apart is not always easy, but this one can be identified by its three-lobed, basal leaves (not shown), and by tiny bracts (leaflets) on each of the flower stems. It also blooms later than the upland larkspur and is considerably taller. The slim larkspur grows in the Pacific coastal states, and inland to Idaho, Montana and Nevada.

### Tower larkspur
### *Delphinium glaucum* S. Watson*

This larkspur is an impressive, often several-stemmed, mountain plant that may grow to be six feet tall or higher. It grows along streambanks where its many bright blue to purple (or, occasionally, almost white) flowers stand out against surrounding green foliage. Also known as the "dunce-cap" delphinium for its long spurred flowers, its appearance and preference for streambanks help to identify the plant. By way of confirmation, the stems below the flowering portion are "fistulous" (hollow), and its large compound leaves are palmate, made up (usually) of five, three-lobed leaflets. The leaves in some plants are noticeably glandular (sticky). The tower larkspur is native to all four northwestern states, north into British Columbia and through the Rocky Mountains to New Mexico.

---

*This plant is usually classified as *Delphinium occidentale* (S. Watson) S. Watson. Present thinking is that *Delphinium occidentale* is a hybrid between this plant, *Delphinium glaucum* which it resembles, and *Delphinium barbeyi* (Huth) Huth (not shown).

### Blue mountain buttercup
### *Ranunculus oresterus* L. D. Benson

The blue mountain buttercup grows from the Blue Mountains of northeastern Oregon, eastward into Idaho and along a swathe across the central part of the state to Elmore (and possibly Camas) County. It blooms, often in large numbers, in moist mountain meadows at lower elevations. The plants are easily distinguished from other buttercups by their clustered appearance, each having five or more flowers, and by their linear, grass-like leaves. The plants are described as having five sepals and petals to a flower, but as can be seen in the illustration, there are often more.

### Plantain-leaved buttercup
### *Ranunculus alismifolius* Geyer ex Benth.
### var. *alismellis* A. Gray

The plantain-leaved buttercup appears soon after snow melt at higher elevations. It is identified by the unusual appearance of its flowers with five (usually) small petals, and by round leaves that bear some resemblance to those of water-plantain (*Alisma* spp., Alismataceae), explaining both common and species names. It is found in most western mountain states, and (rarely) in British Columbia. Several varieties are recognized, identified by the number and size of the petals, by the shape of the leaves, etc.

### Pink buttercup
### *Ranunculus andersonii* A. Gray

The pink buttercup is one that few would recognize as a buttercup at first glance. Its leaves are deeply lobed into frilly leaflets; this, and the unusual pink to reddish-brown color of its petals set it apart from other species. Pink buttercups bloom very early in the spring on well-drained gravelly ground. The plant occurs in central Idaho, eastern Oregon and south to California and Nevada—basically along the western edge of the Intermountain Region. It was first collected by Dr. C. L. Anderson near Carson City, Nevada, in 1866, and named for the doctor by Asa Gray, professor of botany at Harvard University.

### White water buttercup
### *Ranunculus aquatilis* L.

The water buttercup (also "white water-crowfoot") has yellow-centered, mostly five-petaled white flowers whose stalks extend above slow-moving water. Three-parted leaves form when the plants are grown out of water, but when submerged the leaves divide to form soft, hairlike leaflets that offer little resistance to the current. The plants are good indicators of how much dissolved organic material is present—a pond covered with a white blanket of these little plants suggests serious pollution. The water buttercup is found in many western states, north to Canada and Alaska, and in Europe.

### Subalpine buttercup,
### *Ranunculus eschscholtzii* Schltdl.
### var. *trisectus* (Eastw. ex B. L. Rob.) L. D. Benson

The subalpine, or Eschscholtz's, buttercup is a high altitude species, found throughout the western mountains, and north to Alaska. It blooms in moist declivities that catch the snowmelt, often tunneling up through the receding edges of snow fields. The plant is characterized by a thick stem and three-parted leaves. The lobes divide into three segments (not yet developed here). Its flowers have (mostly) five petals and a calyx made up of as many sepals. Several varieties are recognized, ours seems to be var. *trisectus*. Johan Friedrich Eschscholtz (1793–1831) was an Estonian who accompanied Kotzebue's around-the-world-expedition (1815–1818).

### Sage buttercup
### *Ranunculus glaberrimus* Hook.
### var. *ellipticus* (Greene) Greene

Most buttercups are easy to identify generically, but species classification—based in large part on the appearance of their fruit ("achenes")—can be difficult. The sage buttercup is one of the most recognizable because its bright yellow petals have a shiny, waxy gloss; *glaberrimus* means "smoothest." It is a common montane, early spring-blooming plant that favors open sagebrush slopes. The oval leaves of the sage buttercup are often "entire," i.e., they are smooth edged, without lobes or leaflets (although some plants also have three-parted compound leaves). Each plant usually bears several flowers and most have five petals, although the number varies. The sage buttercup is common throughout the West.

### Hillside buttercup
### *Ranunculus jovis* A. Nelson

The hillside, or Jove's buttercup grows on open montane to subalpine sagebrush covered slopes, blooming soon after snowmelt. Its petals are not prominent and some flowers seem not to have any petals. Short-stemmed, lanceolate, three-parted leaves help to identify the plant. Jove's buttercup is found in the intermountain states and in Colorado. The type specimen was collected by Rocky Mountain botanists Ruth Ashton Nelson and Aven Nelson. We have not been able to learn to what or to whom *jovis* refers—presumably to the Roman god, but why?

### Sharp-leaf buttercup
### *Ranunculus acriformis* A. Gray
### var. *montanensis* (Rydb.) L. D. Benson

The sharp-leaf buttercup is a relatively common species that grows at mid-to higher elevations in our mountains. It is usually seen in moist meadows and along streambanks. The plants may be identified by their long-stemmed three-parted compound leaves. Each of the leaflets is further divided into (usually) three slim, pointed lobes. The flowers mostly have five petals, but there are often more. Two varieties are recognized. Those encountered in Idaho grow in the central part of the state, west to Montana and south to Wyoming and Colorado. Another variety, var. *acriformis*, with shorter leaves, grows only in Wyoming and Colorado.

### Globeflower
### *Trollius albiflorus* (A. Gray)
### Rydb.

*Trollius* was derived from the Swiss-German name *trollblume* for the closely related globeflower *Trollius laxus*. The latter is a circumboreal plant that also grows in Asia and Europe (our species is probably a variant of that plant). *Trollius albiflorus* is found in the Canadian provinces of British Columbia and Alberta, south to Washington, Idaho, Wyoming, Utah, and Colorado. It blooms very early, on south facing slopes, as winter turns into spring—globeflowers are often the first flowers to appear while the ground is still mostly snow-covered. Its basal leaves are palmately lobed and toothed, although they are usually not out when the flowers open.

### Western meadowrue
### *Thalictrum occidentale* A. Gray

Thalictrums are found throughout the United States and Canada, but this species occurs only in the West. Its leaves are three-lobed and this species is dioecious with separate male and female plants. Male plants are distinguished by fringe-like dependent anthers (far left). Female plants have wispy pinkish petals (near left). Meadowrues provide ground-cover in shady woods, and are sometimes grown in shaded gardens. *Thaliktron* was used by Dioscorides for a Greek plant, and later became attached to this genus. True rue is an unrelated evergreen shrub, *Ruta graveolens*, with an unpleasant aromatic odor. Our plants have a similar odor, so they became "meadowrues." Western meadowrue was first collected by the explorer Captain John Charles Frémont (1830-1890) in Wyoming in 1843.

### False bugbane,
### *Trautvetteria carolinensis* (Walter) Vail

The false bugbane, as its scientific name suggests, is the same annual plant as one that grows in the southeastern United States. It prefers shaded streambanks and moist forests where the ground is often covered with their large maple-leaf shaped leaves. The flowers are small and gathered into clusters. The generic name, *Trautvetteria*, honors Russian botanist Ernest Rudolf van Trautvetter (1809-1889). Our plant resembles the true bugbane, a related European ornamental, *Cimicifuga foetida* L. used in the past as an insect repellant. The trautvettaria shown here was photographed in the DeVoto Grove, a few miles west of the Lolo Pass summit. The tree is one of the grove's magnificent western red cedars, *Thuja plicata*.

## Buckthorn Family (Rhamnaceae)

The buckthorn family is made up worldwide of 58 genera and 875 species. Most are tropical shrubs or small trees, although it is represented in Idaho by plants belonging to two genera, *Rhamnus* and *Frangula*. All of the Rhamnaceae have bark that acts as a potent purgative. Other than the occasional use of our plants as ornamental shrubs, the purgative value of *Frangula purshiana* bark (cascara, described below) makes it the only American member of the family to have commercial value. Elsewhere the bark and berries of various buckthorns have supplied dyes used in painting and for textiles. The word *rhamnus* from which the family name was derived is an ancient term used for a now unknown species of thorny shrub or tree.

### Tobacco brush (left)
### *Ceanothus velutinus* Douglas ex Hook.

The tobacco brush is common in our mountains. It has many other names, including "mountain-balm," "sticky laurel," "buckbrush," "greasewood," and just plain "ceanothus" (those who would standardize common names suggest "snowbrush ceanothus" for the plant). It is recognized by its foamy clusters of small flowers and leathery, oval, three-veined leaves. The flowers have a distinctive odor that fills the air when many are blooming. While not exactly unpleasant, it is not pleasant either, vaguely reminiscent of the smell of tobacco—whence its common name. The plant grows in most of our western mountain states to subalpine elevations. The closely related *Ceanothus sanguineus* Pursh (redstem ceanothus, or Oregon teatree) is important in forest reclamation, for the plants spring up on burned ground where its seeds have remained dormant for years, until activated by the heat of a wildfire.

### Cascara (center, below left)
### *Frangula purshiana* (DC.) Cooper

Cascara is a small tree with strongly ribbed deep green leaves, small white flowers and sparse blue fruit (berries). It is an attractive plant, and that is probably why Meriwether Lewis gathered it near today's Kamiah, Idaho, on May 29, 1806. Lewis made no mention of the bark's purgative value—apparently the region's Nez Perce Indians were unaware of this. Native Americans in California knew about cascara, however, and told Spanish priests about its laxative effect—explaining why the bark is known medically as *cascara sagrada* (Spanish for "sacred bark"). The trees were scarce for a while in Idaho because so many were harvested for the bark. They are now grown commercially, and once again are found in fair numbers along the Clearwater River where these were photographed. Frederick Pursh named the plant but the name he gave it was already in use. When reclassified, Pursh's name was used as the specific epithet to honor his role in classifying Lewis and Clark plants. Until recently, cascara was classified as a species of *Rhamnus* and is still so listed in many guide books. The generic name *Frangula* was derived from the Latin *frangere* meaning "to break" for the brittle twigs of some species (cf. also our word "fracture").

# Rose Family (Rosaceae)

The rose family is large, made up of 110 genera and 3,100 species. It is well represented in our mountains by plants that range in size from tiny-flowered alpine plants (*Sibbaldia, Kelseya*), to full-sized trees. We have several species of wild rose (*Rosa* spp.) that most anyone will recognize immediately, other plants in the family, however, bear little resemblance to roses. There are, of course, similarities. The Rosaceae have in common five sepals united at the base of the flower to form a disk or cup ("hypanthium" or "hypan") to which the petals (also usually five) and stamens (mostly many) are attached. Most species also have sepal-like leaves or "bracteoles" that arise from the stem just below the flowers. Fruit in the rose family takes many forms: "drupes" as in the genus *Prunus* (plums, apricots, almonds, peaches, cherries, etc.) and "pomes" as in the genera *Malus, Pyrus, Cydonia and Eriobotrya* (apples, pears, quinces, loquats). Some members of the family form multiple small "achenes" (seeds) or "drupelets" which mature into aggregate fruits such as species of *Rubus* (raspberries, blackberries, and similar plants); and *Fragaria* (strawberries). Many of the Rosaceae are also economically important as garden ornamentals. Roses, from which the family's scientific name was derived, have been known by that, or a similar, name in European languages as far back as ancient Greece (the island of Rhodes [*Rodos*] may have taken its name from a related, or similar, flower).

### Western serviceberry
### *Amelanchier alnifolia*
### (Nutt.) Nutt. ex M. Roemer

The western serviceberry (also Saskatoon service-berry) is an attractive small tree that grows throughout northern North America to mid-elevations. The species name *alnifolia*, means "alder-like leaf." Its deep blue berries are edible, although they have little taste. Lewis and Clark collected a variety of the western serviceberry, var. *semiintegrifolia*, at The Dalles in Oregon, and then, what may have been this plant, var. *alnifolia*, in north central Idaho in the spring of 1806. The name *Amelanchier* is derived from a Savoyard term for the medlar-tree. *Mespilus germanica.*

### Black hawthorn
### *Crataegus douglasii* Lindl.

The black hawthorn is found from the Dakotas to the Northwest, growing to fairly high elevations. The trees may be identified by their long, sharp thorns, rounded leaves with scalloped ends, their clusters of white spring-blooming flowers, and later by their dark-red, drying to black, fruit. The gnarled trees have a heavy bark and grow as much as thirty feet high. Palatable, but hardly delicious, "haws" were an important food for Native Americans. Both this, and the similar red hawthorn, *Crataegus chrysocarpa*, grow in Idaho—the latter as a cultivated plant.

### Mountain ash
### *Sorbus scopulinus* Greene

Species of mountain ash—unrelated to the true ash of the eastern United States (*Fraxinus* spp.) are found in many parts of the West. Ours is a small tree that bears clusters of white flowers in late spring, ripening in late summer into colorful bunches of orange berries. Lewis and Clark collected a fruiting specimen in 1805, during their journey west (September 2nd, on the North Fork of the Salmon River) and again on Lolo Pass during their homeward journey (June 27, 1806). The closely related and very similar Sitka mountain ash, *Sorbus sitchensis*, is also found in Idaho, although at higher elevations.

### Western chokecherry
### *Prunus virginiana* L. var. *melanocarpa*
### (A. Nelson) Sarg.

The chokecherry grows in all Canadian provinces, and throughout the United States except for the deep south. The western variety, var. *melanocarpa*—the term means "black fruit"—is a tall bush that flowerswhen it is only a foot or so tall. The plants usually mature as tall bushes; rarely they grow as trees—we have seen them as much as twenty feet high, although this is unusual.

The eastern variety, var. *virginiana* differs in that it is a sizeable tree that does not flower until it is mature. The tart, but edible cherries are "drupes," fleshy fruit, with seed-containing pits. Lewis and Clark gathered specimens of western chokecherry twice, first in September of 1804 in today's South Dakota, and again on May 29, 1806, while camped on the Clearwater River in today's Idaho.

### American plum
### *Prunus americana* Marshall

The American wild plum is widely distributed, found in almost all of the United States with the exception of Oregon, Nevada, Texas and California. The tree shown here was photographed in the foothills of the Clearwater Mountains near Harpster, Idaho.* The American wild plum is the tastiest of all of our native *Prunus* species. As seen in the photographs, early blooming flowers are arranged in an attractive cluster that appears before the leaves are out. The fruit may be yellow, orange, or even, occasionally red. Its lanceolate, serrated leaves are typical of *Prunus* species in general.

---

*The trees in this region may have been planted by settlers; nevertheless, native American plums grow in western Montana, not far from where this specimen was photographed.

### Shrubby cinquefoil
### *Dasiphora fruticosa* (L.) Rydb.

The shrubby cinquefoil is found in most of our northern states and throughout Canada. It may bloom from early summer through August, so it is a favorite with landscape gardeners who know it as "potentilla." You'll see shrubby cinquefoil blooming on sagebrush slopes, high on alpine tundra, and in cities as an ornamental plant. *Dasiphora* from the Greek implies "thick foliage," *floribunda* from the Latin means "many flowers," and "cinquefoil," from the French, means "five-leaved," for the plant's five-fingered leaves (an older name, "golden hardhack," has been suggested as a common name for the plant). Meriwether Lewis collected a specimen of shrubby cinquefoil along Montana's Blackfoot River on July 6, 1806.

### Bitterbrush
### *Purshia tridentata* (Pursh) DC.

The bitterbrush (also antelope-brush) grows throughout the West. It can be confused with the shrubby cinquefoil, although it blooms earlier, has smaller, quite different flowers, and three-toothed (*tridentata*) leaves. The plant is usually found with sagebrush and may grow quite high in our mountains. It is an important browse plant for deer and antelope. Like the shrubby cinquefoil, the bitter-brush makes a good ornamental, although—because it blooms for a much shorter time— is less commonly used for that purpose. The name *Purshia* honors Frederick Pursh (1774-1820) the botanist who classified specimens returned by the Lewis and Clark expedition. Meriwether Lewis collected the plant on the same day as the shrubby cinquefoil.

### Hillside ocean spray
### *Holodiscus discolor* (Pursh) Maxim.

Each spring the Clearwater River Gorge is alive with ocean spray shrubs in bloom—and they would have been in bloom while Lewis and Clark were camped nearby, in today's Kamiah. Most likely it was Meriwether Lewis who collected a specimen on May 29, 1806. Ocean spray grows throughout the West, from British Columbia to Texas and south to South America. As the illustrations shows, it is an attractive spring-blooming bush whose dependent clusters of tiny off-white flowers make a handsome ornamental plant. The scientific name, *Holodiscus discolor*, with its two "discs," is easily explained. The first "disc" in the generic name refers to the flower's annular disk or "hypanthium," a family characteristic. The second "disc" in *discolor* refers to its two-colored leaves, green on top and silvery gray beneath.

### Mallow-leaf ninebark
### *Physocarpus malvaceus* (Greene) Kuntze

The mallow-leaf ninebark is a common shrub in our mountains, growing to fairly high elevations. Circumscribed clusters ("corymbs") of flowers grow on the ends of many small branches; these, as well as the plant's rough and peeling bark (whence "ninebark"), help to identify it. The species name *malvaceus* means "mallow-like," as the leaves are similar to those of some mallows (although the leaves might also be referred to as "maple-leaf-like"). Interestingly, Meriwether Lewis several times mentioned seeing "nine-bark" (or "seven-bark"), a plant he knew from the East.

### Common raspberry
### *Rubus idaeus* L. var. *strigosus* (Michx.) Maxim.

The wild raspberry is one of the most widely distributed members of the rose family, found throughout North America (save in a few southern states) as well as in Eurasia. The plants are quite at home in our mountains and grow at least as high as treeline. Spring-blooming five-petaled, small white flowers are typical of those of most *Rubus* species. The berries do tend to be smaller than domestic fruit—hardly surprising for they grow on unfertilized rocky ground. Nevertheless, if you sample the ripe fruit you will find that it is the same plant as the delicious raspberries that grow in our gardens.

### Thimbleberry
### *Rubus parviflorus* Nutt.

The thimbleberry is common in Idaho's mountains, growing as an "unarmed" (lacking brambles) shrub that may be six feet or more high. The plants are easily recognized by their large, deep-green, maple-like leaves, by their large white blossoms (up to 2" across), and by their raspberry-like fruit. The fruit—unlike that of raspberries—is disappointingly tasteless. Lewis and Clark collected the thimbleberry on April 15, 1806, while near today's The Dalles, Oregon. Unfortunately, their specimen was in poor condition on its return to the United States, so it could not be published as a new species. Thomas Nuttall later found the plant on Mackinac Island, in Lake Huron, and gave it the species name *parviflorus* ("small-flower"), a strange choice, for its flowers are the largest of any of our native *Rubus* species.

### Nootka rose (left, left center)
### *Rosa nutkana* C. Presl
### var. *hispida* Fernald

The Nootka rose is named for the Nootka Sound on Vancouver Island where it was first collected by a botanist with the Malaspina Spanish expedition (1791), although it was not described until much later. Our plant's varietal name, *hispida*, means "bristly." It grows to six feet or more, usually in well watered places. The flowers of wild roses are quite similar, so other criteria are used to identify the various species. This plant's compound leaves have three to seven leaflets and are edged with fine teeth. The fruit, "rose-hips," may be used as an emergency food, although they're unpalatable, consisting more of seed than pulp; that does not discourage the birds that eat them. The berries are rich in vitamin C, a benefit of "rosehip tea," used in folk medicine to treat various ailments. There are three varieties of *Rosa nutkana*; ours grows chiefly east of the Cascades, whereas var. *nutkana* grows further west and north. There is another, as yet unnamed variety that occurs mostly in the southern Rocky Mountains.

Another common species, Wood's Rose, *Rosa woodsii* Lindl., (not illustrated) has leaves and flowers similar to those of the Nootka rose, although it is a smaller and less robust shrub. While it grows as high as the foothills, it is mostly a lowland plant found throughout western United States and Canada, east to the Mississippi River. It also is made up of several varieties.

### Subalpine spiraea (left)
### *Spiraea splendens*
### Baumann ex K. Koch.

The subalpine spiraea is a low shrub characterized by dense clusters of tiny pink flowers. Its deciduous leaves are simple and edged with fine teeth. The plant grows only in the mountains of the Northwest, and in California and Nevada, usually on rocky ground and often in moist places. There are many species of spiraea; understandably these attractive plants are often planted in ornamental gardens.

## Prairie smoke
### *Geum triflorum* Pursh
### var. *ciliatum* (Pursh) Fassett

Prairie smoke flowers, with their nodding, vase-like shape, reddish color and recurved bracteoles (accessory sepal-like leaves) are unique. The plants grow as high as treeline, blooming in mid- to late spring, often in large patches. *Geum* is an old Latin name for plants in this genus. The species name, *triflorum*, describes the plant's three-to-a-stem flowers. Imagine a patch of fruiting plants (right) and you'll to see how the common names "prairie smoke" and "old man's whiskers" were derived. Lewis and Clark gathered this plant—previously unknown to science—near Idaho's Weippe Prairie on June 12, 1806. *Geum triflorum* grows all across northern North America as far east as Wisconsin and Ontario.

## Ross's avens
### *Geum rossii* (R. Br.) Ser.
### var. *turbinatum* (Rydb.) C. L. Hitchc.

Ross's avens is a subalpine or alpine plant that is at home on rocky tundra. Its pinnatifid (feather-like) leaves help to identify the plant as do purple-tinged stems and calyces. Several varieties have been described, but this is the only one found in Idaho. The plant occurs in other western mountain states, also at high elevations. The species name honors the arctic explorer Sir James Clark Ross (1800-1862). The varietal name, *turbinatum*, refers to the raised central disk.

### Gordon's ivesia
### *Ivesia gordonii* (Hook.) Torr. & A. Gray

Gordon's ivesia is found at high elevations throughout Idaho. The plants' pale yellow flowers are clustered into heads on the end of each of several long stems. The petals are glossy giving the flower heads an overall glistening appearance. The central portion of the flower—the "hypan"—is raised, and often plumped up, or "turbinate." The leaves are pinnate, made up of very closely ranked small leaflets. Once one knows the plant, it is surprising how often it is encountered growing on rocky alpine terrain. It is found in the northern and central Rocky Mountains, west to the coastal ranges. Four varieties occur in Idaho. The plant in the illustration, var. *ursinorum* (Jeps.) Ertter & Reveal, grows in the southern half of the state (the tall plant in the background is an unidentified composite). Dr. Eli Ives (1779-1861) for whom the genus was named was a botanist and physician. A similar plant, *Ivesia tweedyi* Rydb. is rare; it grows in mountains near Coeur d'Alene.

### Kelseya
### *Kelseya uniflora* (S. Watson) Rydb.

The kelseya is an early flowering, mat-forming plant that grows above treeline in the mountains of Idaho, Wyoming, Colorado, and Montana (where it may grow at lower altitudes). It is the only plant in its genus. Surprisingly, even though the kelseya is uncommon, it has been cultivated as an "alpine" in rock gardens throughout the world. One can understand why it is popular with rock gardeners, for it is an exotic and attractive little plant that spreads over rocks, forming a carpet of tiny blue-gray leaves dotted with minute pink and white flowers. The flowers—shown greatly magnified here—at first glance seem to be no larger than the head of a large pin.

*Kelseya uniflora* is named for Rev. Frank Duncan Kelsey (1849-1905), a resident of Helena, Montana (and later of Toledo, Ohio) who first collected the plant.

### Cliff drymocallis
***Drymocallis pseudorupestris*** (Rydb.) Rydb. var. *saxicola* Ertter

Until recently, this wildflower was classified as *Potentilla glandulosa* Lindl. with the common name "sticky cinquefoil." Recent studies, however, have shown that it is not related to the potentillas—not surprising, given its white flowers and pinnate leaves. Var. *saxicola*, common in Idaho, grows as high as treeline where its size is reduced (right). The species, as one or another of many varieties, is found in most states and provinces west of the Mississippi River. The name *drymocallis*, from the Greek, means "wood beauty"; the Latin name, *saxicola*, means "mountain (or cliff) dwelling.," reflecting this variety's growth preference.

### Slender cinquefoil
***Potentilla gracilis*** Douglas ex Hook.

The slender cinquefoil is one of the most variable of all potentillas. It grows throughout the west, as far east as the Dakotas, all across Canada and into Alaska. There are several varieties, characterized by differences in their leaves—how deeply indented the lobes of the leaflets are, how much hair grows on their surface, etc.—differences mostly of importance to botanists. All have palmately compound leaves with five to nine toothed pinnate (feather-like) leaflets and five-petaled yellow flowers with a central disk, typical of the rose family. The species name, *gracilis*, means "slender." The plant in the illustration is var. *elmeri* (Rydb) Jeps.

### Early cinquefoil
***Potentilla concinna*** Richards.

The early cinquefoil is one of several quite similar, low-growing potentillas that are found high in our mountains. Its leaves vary from digitate (as shown here) to pinnate. The individual leaflets are toothed at the ends. It may be distinguished by its leaves, for their undersurfaces are covered with downy, whitish hairs—they are "tomentose." The early cinquefoil grows from the central Canadian provinces, through the Rocky Mountain states to Arizona and New Mexico, west to Nevada and east to the Dakotas. It was collected in 1820 by John Richardson, physician-naturalist with the first Franklin expedition, at Fort Carlton on the Saskatchewan River in Canada. The name *concinnus*, from the Latin, means "neat."

## Sheep cinquefoil
### *Potentilla ovina*
### Macoun ex J. M. Macoun

The sheep cinquefoil has—at least for the amateur botanist—a good thing going for it; its leaves are unusual for a potentilla making it easy to recognize. It is a small creeping plant that grows from montane to alpine elevations. Pinnate leaves arise mostly from the base of the plant and have small, tightly ranked, furred leaflets. The yellow flowers are similar to those of other potentillas. It is said that Macoun, who described this plant, found it on Sheep Mountain in British Columbia, and gave it the name *ovina*, a word that means "of sheep." The plant is found all through the Rocky Mountains and west to mountain ranges in Oregon.

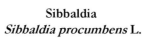

## Sibbaldia
### *Sibbaldia procumbens* L.

*Sibbaldia procumbens* is the only North American plant in its genus (although five other species occur in Eurasia). As is often the case, when the author of one of our plants is designated as "L." (for Linnaeus), the plant is found in both the Old and New Worlds. The sibbaldia is an alpine plant in the United States, growing at progressively lower elevations north to Siberia, Alaska, across Canada to Labrador and Greenland. Sibbaldias—the common name, "creeping-glow-wort" has also been suggested—are dwarf plants, far smaller than the illustration suggests. They may be identified by tiny flowers borne in small clusters along and at the ends of stout stems. The flowers have five prominent sepals and five narrowly attached petals. Basal leaves are strawberry-like, with several teeth at the end of each of three leaflets. The plants spread by creeping rhizomes. Sir Robert Sibbald (1641-1722) was a prominent physician of Edinburgh with a strong interest in botany. He published a natural history of Scotland in which he described various plants, including this one. When Linnaeus described it, he took note of Sibbald's contribution, naming it *Sibbaldia*.

### Wild strawberry
### *Fragaria virginiana* Mill var. *glauca* (S. Watson) Staudt

Wild strawberries are found in every part of North America. Common in our mountains, they occur at all elevations, even above treeline. Their flowers are large, with five separated petals, and many anthers and stigmas arising from a central receptacle. Fruiting plants are not common, but when encountered, are unmistakably strawberries, in taste and appearance. Two varieties occur in Idaho. The plant shown here has smooth, almost hairless leaves. The other variety, var. *platypetala*, has larger flowers and furry leaves and stems. The name, *Fragaria*, was derived from *fraga* the Latin word for "strawberry."

### Western burnet
### *Sanguisorba annua* (Nutt.) Nutt.

The western burnet has dense clusters of tiny flowers borne, usually, on several branching stems. Although not well shown in the illustration, the stem is leafy, especially in its lower part. The compound, pinnate leaves are fern-like. The burnet prefers open fields and grows in our mountains at least as high as the montane zone. The common name "burnet" has been used for centuries for a European species; the word means "brown," reflecting the color of post-mature flowerheads. *Sanguisorba*, in turn, implies "blood absorbing" as the plants apparently were, in the past, thought to have styptic properties. Our burnet is found from British Columbia to California, east to Nevada, Utah, Idaho and Montana.

# Madder Family (Rubiaceae)

Although only a few Rubiaceae grow in Idaho, the family is a moderately large one consisting of over 650 genera and some 13,000 species. Almost all—trees, shrubs, vines and a few herbaceous plants—are native to the tropics. Family characteristics include square stems, opposing narrow leaves usually arranged as whorls at intervals along the stem, and small four or five petaled flowers. Some contain alkaloidal substances that are important to man. These include quinine (*Cinchona* spp.) and ipecac (*Psychotria emetica*)—both from South American trees; yohimbine derived from an African tree (*Corynanthe johimbe*), used to treat impotence and as a topical vasodilator in surgery; and coffee from the fruit of various species of *Coffea* (Africa). Some of our most important garden ornamentals are also in the madder family: *Gardenia, Penta, Ixora,* and others. Finally, the red dye madder from which the family takes its common name—and indirectly its scientific name—was also obtained from species of Rubiaceae.

The word "madder" has been applied to a red vegetable dye in use since prehistoric times. While the dye is found in the roots of other Rubiaceae, (*Galium, Asperula*), the greatest concentrations occur in species of *Rubia,* from which the family name Rubiaceae was derived (*rubus* is Latin for "red"). "Dyer's madder," used to dye fabrics, and the artists' pigment "rose-madder" was extracted from the European plant *Rubia tinctorum,* and from *Rubia cordifolium,* an Asian plant. In the second half of the nineteenth century, madder dyes—alizarin and purpurin—were synthesized so plant madder is seldom used today.

The bedstraws (*Galium* spp.) are sweet smelling Rubiaceae that dry to give a springy stuffing used in the past for pillows and mattresses, whence their common name. "Cleavers" is another name for bedstraws, one that conjures up mental pictures of a wicked kitchen utensil. "To cleave" is an Old English word, however, one that means "to stick" or "adhere" (cf. the injunction "cleave unto me"), this because the seeds, stems, and branches of some bedstraws attach themselves to passersby.

### Fragrant bedstraw
### *Galium triflorum* Michx.

The fragrant bedstraw scrambles along forest floors, loosely climbing other plants that it encounters. Its bright green, narrow leaves form whorls at intervals along the stems. Small four-petaled flowers, inconsistently borne in groups of three at the end of long stemlets, arise at the leaf nodes. They give off a sweetish grassy odor; one can understand how the dried plants of this and related species might make pleasant smelling bedstraw for pillows and mattresses. The plant's appearance is similar to that of the related European herb, sweet woodruff or waldmeister (*Galium odoratum* Scop.), that is steeped in white wine to make May wine. *Galium triflorum* is a circumboreal plant that is found throughout North America and as far south as Mexico.

### Watson's bedstraw
### *Galium watsonii* (A. Gray) A. Heller

Watson's bedstaw is an atypical galium, covered with long bristly hairs. The plant blooms in the summer, favoring high dry places. The flowers of most bedstraws are small and quite unremarkable. This plant's light yellow, four-petaled flowers are also small, but long bristles originating on the flowers' ovaries protrude to give it a brush-like appearance (the plants are dioecious—the male plants are not so hairy). The name *Galium* is derived from the Greek *gala* for "milk" (cf. "galaxy" for the milky way), because the European yellow bedstraw (*Galium verum* L.) curdles milk and formerly was used as vegetable rennet in cheese-making, imparting the plants' yellow color to the finished product (nowadays rennet derived from the lining of calves' stomachs is used for the same purpose and the yellow color is often an added food dye). Unlike the plant shown above, this ones' range is restricted. It occurs from Washington to California, and east to northwestern Nevada and into Idaho.

**Northern bedstraw**
***Galium boreale* L.**

The northern bedstraw is an ubiquitous circumpolar plant found in all of the United States (save in a few southern states), Canada, Greenland and Eurasia. The plants are many-branched with four lanceolate leaves arising from stem nodes. Dense clusters ("cymose panicles") of small four-petaled white flowers are borne on stemlets given off from leaf nodes at the top of the stems, producing, overall, a showy profusion. The plants grow at all elevations, from sea-level to tree-line, preferring moist situations. (The background yellow composites are a species of *Arnica*.)

# Saxifrage Family (Saxifragaceae)

The word "saxifrage" is derived from the Latin *frango* meaning "I break" and *saxum* meaning "rock." Pliny (b. 23 AD, died 79 A.D. in the eruption of Vesuvius) in his *Natural History*, wrote that the name *saxifragum* (the Latin word means "stone-breaker") referred to the plant's supposed ability to dissolve kidney and bladder stones. More likely, however, it reflected the plants' growth habit, for saxifrages often grow in rocky clefts, seemingly having broken the stone apart. The family is not a large one, consisting of about 30 genera and 325 species. The plants are mostly herbaceous (non-woody). Although the family is distributed throughout the world, most members are found in the north temperate zone, often in inhospitable surroundings (desert, arctic, alpine, bogs and as aquatic forms). The family has little economic importance, although a few are used in folk medicine and others find a place in ornamental gardens. Saxifrage flowers usually have five sepals, five petals, and ten stamens. As will be seen on the following pages, many plants in this family have clusters of small flowers borne atop a long stem with a basal rosette of toothed leaves, an identifying feature. Finally, note that although we are incuding *Parnassia fimbriata*, the fringed grass-of-Parnassus, with the saxifrage family, it is now classified as belonging to its own family, Parnassiaceae.

### Gooseberry-leaved alumroot
### *Heuchera grossulariifolia* Rydb.

The gooseberry-leaved alumroot blooms from late spring well into the summer, favoring cliffsides (where it usually grows as a solitary plant) and on rocky ground (where it may grow in clusters) from mid-elevations to alpine tundra. The species name is derived from the resemblance of its leaves to those of gooseberries in the currant family (Grossulariaceae).* Its small flowers have five sepals joined to form a bell-shaped receptacle that almost hides the petals. The popular name, alumroot, is derived from its puckery taste, for the roots and stems contain a high concentration of tannin. The generic name honors Johann Heinrich von Heucher (1677-1747), Professor of Medicine at Wittenberg in Germany. It is unlikely that Heucher knew this plant, for it is not found in Europe. Linnaeus, in his *Species Plantarum* (1753) often gave plants the names of prominent men who had nothing to do with their namesakes. This, and the poker alumroot shown below are both plants of the northern Rockies, and Pacific coastal ranges.

---

*At one time, members of the gooseberry family, Grossulariaceae, were classified as Saxifragaceae, so it is not surprising that the plants bear some resemblance.

### Poker alumroot
### *Heuchera cylindrica* Douglas ex Hook.

The poker alumroot is quite similar in appearance and in growth habit to the gooseberry leaved alumroot shown above, differing mainly in the shape of its leaves. These tend to be round with shallow lobes. There is considerable difference in this plant's morphology from place to place and even from plant to plant, and six different varieties are sometimes recognized; these have relatively minor variations in leaf shape. Unlike *Heuchera grossularifolia* shown above, petals are sometimes absent in the flowers of this species.

**Smallflower woodlandstar**
*Lithophragma parviflorum* (Hook.) Nutt. ex Torr. & A. Gray

The woodlandstars (also "prairiestars") illustrated here are two of the three species often seen in our mountains. All are quite similar; showy white (occasionally pale pink) flowers are about half an inch in diameter, but they are eye-catchers, thanks to their cleft petals. Prominent calyces with five pointed tips cup the flowers. Five deeply cleft petals have, depending on the species, three, five, or seven lobes. Small flower clusters are borne atop long, usually reddish to purple colored stems that arise from a basal cluster of lobed leaves. Woodland stars are montane plants, scattered in generous numbers in sagebrush, in mountain meadows, and along stream banks, where they bloom into the summer at higher elevations. This species is found in British Columbia and Alberta, south to California, Nevada, central Utah, northern Colorado and northwestern Nebraska.

**Bulbous woodlandstar**
*Lithophragma glabrum* Nutt.

The bulbous woodlandstar (also prairiestar) was until recently classified as *Lithophragma bulbifera* Rydberg. The plant often forms tiny bulbs at the base of the flowers and leaves and these sometimes replace these structures. The bulbous prairiestar's petals are rather attenuated and usually have five deeply dissected lobes, unlike the woodlandstar shown above. It also tends to bloom earlier in the spring than other species. The genus name, *Lithophragma* is derived from the Greek *lithos* for "stone" and *phragma* meaning "wall," from the plants' tendency to grow in rocky places. While bulbils are common in this species, other woodlandstars may, on occasion, also produce them. In addition to those that form above ground, subterranean bulbils may also form, and are probably more effective in creating new plants than are above-ground bulbils and seeds.

**Five-stamen mitrewort**
***Mitella pentandra* Hook. (left above)**
**Side-flowered mitrewort**
***Mitella stauropetala* Piper (left center)**

The five-stamen (or alpine) mitella, *Mitella pentandra* and the side-flowered mitella, *Mitella stauropetala* (from *stavros* a Greek word for "cross," reflecting the shape of the attenuated petals) are two of the four species of *Mitella* found in Idaho. The side-flowered mitrewort grows in Idaho, west to Oregon and Washington, east into Montana and Wyoming, south into Utah and western Colorado. The five-stamen mitella has much the same distribution in the United States but also ranges as far north as Alaska and the neighboring Canadian provinces, and south to California and Nevada. Both prefer moist environments and are usually found in shaded woods and along stream banks. As with many other plants in the saxifrage family, the plants' basal leaves are disproportionately large when compared to the tiny flowers (the flowers are greatly magnified in these illustrations). The bizarre little flowers with their five skeletal petals should be easy to identify the first time they are seen. The word "mitella" is a diminutive form of the Latin *mitra* ("hat" or "cap"), a reflection of the shape of the plants' fruiting body said to resemble a bishop's hat.

**Threeleaf foamflower**
***Tiarella trifoliata* L. var. *unifoliata* (Hook.) Kurtz**

The threeleaf foamflower (also known as the coolwort, and the laceflower) ranges from Alaska, south to California, east to Alberta and across Idaho to Montana. It too prefers deep woods and well-shaded stream banks. Tiny, white, five-petaled flowers are borne in small clusters ("panicles") on stemlets arising from a single long stem. The varietal name, *unifoliata*, differentiates this variety from var. *trifoliata* in which the leaves are divided into three separate leaflets, rather than the single, lobed leaves of the plant shown here.

**Brook saxifrage**
***Saxifraga odontoloma* Piper**

The brook, or streambank, saxifrage, formerly *Saxifraga arguta*, is typical of plants in the genus *Saxifraga*. Most have a basal cluster of leaves and a long stem bearing many small flowers. The brook saxifrage is a common plant in our mountains, often turning stream banks green with its leaves. The plants are easily identified by their attractive, bright green, deeply scalloped, oval or fan-shaped leaves. These give the plant both its old and new species name (both mean "toothed"). The brook saxifrage is able to thrive in varying light intensities, growing equally well in bright sunlight or deep shade. It is found in all of the western mountains from Alaska southward to Mexico.

**Mountain saxifrage**
***Saxifraga occidentalis* S. Watson**

In the past, this species was made up of a half dozen varieties, each with slightly different characteristics and territories. Recently, however, these have been reclassified, leaving *Saxifraga occidentalis* as its own, well-defined, species. The plant blooms in early summer, preferring the moist ground of mountain meadows and the banks of mountain lakes. It may be identified by a stem that gives off many stemlets each bearing a cluster of white flowers. Each flower has two prominent red carpals that mature into a two-parted capsule ("follicle"). The plant is native to the Rocky Mountains, south to New Mexico, as well as in the four northwestern states. It is also found in Alberta and British Columbia. Several other saxifrages very similar in appearance to this one also occur in our mountains.

# Saxifragaceae (Parnassiaceae)

## Purple saxifrage
### *Saxifraga oppositifolia* L.

The purple saxifrage forms dense cushions on the rocky ground of alpine tundra. The flowers, on almost non-existent stems, bloom while there is snow on nearby slopes. Its tiny, opposite leaves are tightly arrayed. Striking pink to purple, five-petaled flowers range up to an inch in diameter. This is a circumboreal arctic/alpine plant found high in the mountains of the Northwest, Wyoming, and north to Alaska. Several varieties are recognized and one or another may be found all across northern Canada to Labrador as well as on arctic islands, Greenland and in the alpine ranges of the Old World.

## Fringed grass-of-Parnassus
### *Parnassia fimbriata* K. D. Koenig

*Parnassia* species were, until recently, in the saxifrage family. The genus now makes up its own family, Parnassiaceae. *Parnassia palustris* L., a circumboreal, subalpine and alpine plant that grows throughout the northern hemisphere (including northern Idaho) is the original grass-of-Parnasssus. The name was given by Dioscorides who associated the plant with the Parnassus Range in Greece, where it is found today. Our plant, *Parnassia fimbriata*, is almost identical except for its fringed ("fimbriated") petals. It blooms, from mid-summer on, in swampy mountain meadows, and along the banks of slow moving streams, at montane to alpine elevations. It is easily identified, for the plants have single white flowers atop naked stems that emerge from basal clumps of kidney-shaped leaves. The flower's five-veined petals are fringed for about half their length. Five stamens emerging from between the petals are tipped with club-like yellow anthers. A yellow "staminode"—a modified, sterile, yellow nectar-secreting stamen—is located at the base of each petal.

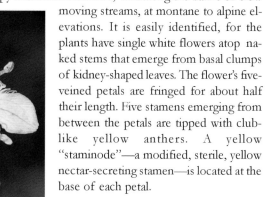

# Figwort or Snapdragon Family (Scrophulariaceae)

Because the figwort, a Eurasian plant, is not well known in America, the Scrophulariaceae family is sometimes referred to as the snapdragon family. Recently, with the advent of DNA studies, many plants previously classified as Scrophulariaceae have been reassigned to other plant families. Understandably, this is confusing for those who grew up using the older classifications. Despite these changes, various plants formerly classified as Scrophulariaceae do have common characteristics. These include: flowers that mostly have five petals joined for much of their length; a "lip" formed by prominent lower petals; usually four anthers (although some genera—notably *Penstemon*—have a sterile fifth stamen).

The family, as originally classified, is a large one that included approximately 5,100 species spread throughout the world. Despite its size, its members have little economic importance other than as ornamentals (*Digitalis purpurea* is an exception; not only is it a popular garden plant, but the leaves are the source of digitalis, a potent and useful cardiac stimulant). In order to simplify taxonomic matters insofar as possible, we have elected to place all of the plants previously classified as Scrophulariaceae under that heading, while including the newer—now generally accepted—classifications as subheadings. These include:

(1) The broomrape family, Orobanchaceae, includes the broomrapes (*Orobanche*), the paintbrushes (*Castilleja*), the owl-clovers (*Orthocarpus*), and the louseworts (*Pedicularis*); all are genera found in our mountains.

(2) Species of monkeyflowers (*Mimulus*) are now classified as Phrymaceae (lop-seed family).

(3) Species of *Penstemon*, *Collinsia*, *Veronica*, *Synthyris* (Kitten-tails), *Chionophila* (snowlovers), and *Linaria* (toadflaxes) are now classified as Plantaginaceae (plantain family).

(4) All of which leaves only one local plant—*Verbascum thapsus*, the common, Eurasian roadside mullein—remaining as a true Scrophulariaceae.

### Western naked broomrape
### *Orobanche uniflora* L.
### var. *occidentalis* R. L. Taylor & MacBryde

The naked broomrape is a non-chlorophyllaceous plant found throughout North America. It is a parasite whose modified root system invades the roots of neighboring plants—usually sagebrush. Lack of chlorophyll results in a yellowish-brown to purple coloration (the latter, as in the inset, is more noticeable at subalpine elevations). The plant's relationship to other hemi-parasitic Scrophulariaceae (*Castilleja, Orthocarpus, Pedicularis,* etc.) has long been noted, and these genera have been reclassified and are now in the broomrape family. The "rape" in "broomrape" was derived from a Latin word, *rapum,* meaning "knob" referring to lumps that form on the roots of brooms (shrubs in the pea family), caused by a European broomrape. *Orobanche,* in turn, was derived from two Greek words and means, approximately, "vetch-strangler."

### Scarlet paintbrush
### *Castilleja miniata*
### Douglas ex Hook.

Note the green flowers among the colorful red bracts. Continued on the following page.

Paintbrushes are mostly found in the American West; about forty species grow in the Northwest: we can only show a representative sampling here. Look closely at a castilleja's terminal bracts and you'll see slim flowers. Each has a four-spiked calyx from which five petals protrude (see the illustration on the previous page). Two lower petals join to form a characteristic "lip"; there are also two tiny lateral petals and an overhanging beaklike fifth petal known as a "galea" (Latin for "helmet"). Paintbrushes are hemi-parasites capable of photosynthesis, but they also require root contact with another plant, usually sagebrush, making them difficult to cultivate.

*Castilleja miniata*, shown here and on the previous page, is the most common paintbrush in Idaho, growing at all elevations to well above treeline. The red bracts (upper leaves) each have two small lateral projections—an identifying feature. David Douglas first collected the plant in Oregon's Blue Mountains. The genus *Castilleja* was named for Spanish botanist Domingo Castillejo (1744-1793).

Other wildflowers in this illustration include mountain bluebell (*Mertensia ciliata*), Lewis's monkeyflower (*Mimulus lewisii*), a species of *Arnica*, monkshood (*Aconitum columbianum*), upland larkspur (*Delphinium nuttallianum*), brook saxifrage (*Saxifraga odontoloma*), and mountain death camas (*Anticlea elegans*). All are described and illustrated elsewhere in this book.
The trees are Douglas fir (*Pseudotsuga menziesii*), and subalpine fir (*Abies lasiocarpa*).

### Western paintbrush
### *Castilleja occidentalis* Torr.

The western (also pale-yellow) paintbrush is a subalpine to alpine species often seen growing in dry surroundings where it favors rocky soil and talus slopes. It has narrow, lanceolate leaves (the uppermost ones are sometimes lobed) borne on woody stems. The bracts are a washed-out pale-yellow to nearly white color. This, in addition to the plants' preference for dry places, helps to identify it. The western sagebrush is a Rocky Mountain plant that grows as far south as New Mexico and north to British Columbia and Alberta.

### Rosy Indian paintbrush
### *Castilleja rhexifolia* Rydb.

The rosy, or rhexia-leaved Indian paintbrush may be identified by its dark-red bracts and by its lanceolate leaves that lack projecting lobes. While not uncommon, the rosy paintbrush is seen less often than the scarlet paintbrush shown on the previous pages. The species name, *rhexifolia,* links the shape of its leaves to those of rhexias, plants found mostly in the southern and eastern states. The rosy paintbrush grows from British Columbia and Alberta, to northeastern Oregon, then south in the Rocky Mountain states to New Mexico  It is usually found in fairly moist situations.

### Sulphur Indian paintbrush
### *Castillea sulphurea* Rydb.

The sulphur Indian paintbrush is closely related to the western paintbush shown above. Both have multiple stems arising from a woody central stem ("caudex"). This plant is distinguished by its yellow leaves and bracts, responsible for the "sulphur" in its common name. Its range, like the related western paintbrush, includes all of the Rocky Mountain states, British Columbia, and Alberta. Disjunct populations are also found in the Black Hills of South Dakota and the Wasatch Mountains of Utah. Most commonly, it is found growing on moist ground.

### Rocky Mountain paintbrush
### *Castilleja covilleana* L. F. Hend.

The Rocky Mountain (or Coville's) paintbrush is a localized plant found in central Idaho and, unusually, in adjacent Montana. Despite its limited range, it is not an uncommon plant in central Idaho. The plant is not hard to identify, given its elongated, spidery, three lobed leaves and bright red, orange, or occasionally yellow bracts. It is one of our earliest blooming paintbrushes, at home on rocky, sagebrush covered slopes. The plant's species name honors a prominent botanist, Frederick Vernon Coville (1867-1937), curator of the U.S. National Herbarium and chief botanist of the USDA.

### Cusick's paintbrush
### *Castilleja cusickii* Greenm.

Cusick's paintbrush is a common montane to alpine plant in Idaho, the surrounding states and British Columbia. The plant's attractive bright yellow bracts, its preference for the mucky ground of moist meadows, and its tendency to grow in discrete clusters should be sufficient to identify the plant when first seen.

### Yellow owl-clover
### *Orthocarpus luteus* Nutt.

The Yellow owl-clover, *Orthocarpus luteus*, is a slender plant with narrow unlobed leaves at the base of the stem, becoming lobed toward the top where they then become the yellow bracts that give the plant both its common and scientific names (*lutea* is Latin for "yellow"). Typically these are a bit sticky to the touch, with fine hairs that impart a grayish color to the leaves. The plant has a much wider distribution than does the thin-leaved owl-clover shown below, as it grows in all of the western states and Canadian provinces as far east as Ontario. The plants are common in montane and subalpine zones.

### Thin-leaf owl-clover
### *Orthocarpus tenuifolius*
### (Pursh) Benth.

Owl-clovers (also "owl's clover") are closely related to Indian paintbrushes—so much so that at one time they were included in the same genus. Most owl-clovers are not particularly attractive, but this one with its delicate yellow and light purple bracts is an exception. It is a montane to alpine plant found in the northern part of Idaho as well as in other northwestern states and in British Columbia. Meriwether Lewis collected this plant on July 1, 1806, while camped at "Traveler's Rest" in the Bitterroot Valley near today's Missoula, Montana. *Orthocarpus* means "straight fruit," referring to the shape of the seed capsule; *tenuifolia* means "thin leaf"—the plant's common name. The origin of the term "owl-clover" is obscure.

### Elephant-head, *Pedicularis groenlandica* Retz.

The elephant-head lousewort (also known as pink elephants and Greenland lousewort) grows in all of our western states and throughout Canada (despite its species name, it is not found in Greenland). This lousewort's bizarre little flowers are borne in a tightly packed spike above feather-like leaves. The flowers have a hooded upper petal, or "galea" with a long projection that resembles an elephant's head and trunk. A three lobed lower lip forms the face. It is a montane to alpine plant that grows on moist ground from late spring to mid-summer. The appearance of the inflorescence is so distinctive that one only has to have heard the common name to recognize the plant. Louseworts, like other Orobanchaceae are to a degree parasites that depend on the presence of other plants. *Pedicularis* is a Latin word meaning "lousy"; in former times it was believed that sheep browsing the European lousewort, *Pedicularis sylvatica* L., were infested with lice from the plant.

*Pedicularis groenlandica* is a Lewis and Clark plant; or, more accurately, a Lewis plant, for the two captains had gone separate ways after crossing the Clearwater Mountains and Bitterroot Range on their return journey. Meriwether Lewis collected the Greenland lousewort on July 6, 1806, on the Blackfoot River, upstream from today's Missoula, Montana.

### White sickletop lousewort
### *Pedicularis racemosa* Douglas ex Benth.
### var. *alba* (Pennell) Cronquist

The sickletop lousewort (also parrot's beak lousewort) is another *Pedicularis* species commonly encountered in our high mountain meadows. It grows in most of our western mountain states and adjacent Canadian provinces. The plant shown here, var. *alba*, is white-flowered, common to Idaho, although a pink to purple variety, var. *racemosa*, grows further to the west. One will have no problem identifying either variety, for the galea (a modified upper petal) is sharply hooked into the sickle shape as shown in the illustration, a shape that is responsible for its common names. The species name, *racemosa*, is a description of how the flowers are clustered, botanically as a "raceme."

**Bracted lousewort**
*Pedicularis bracteosa* Benth. var. *siifolia* (Rydb.) Cronquist

The yellow-flowered bracted lousewort (left and foreground above) grows in moist places, at higher altitudes. The species name, *bracteosa,* is derived from small toothed leaves (bracts) that subtend each of its flowers. The plants have fernlike leaves, common to the genus *Pedicularis*. Seven varieties of bracted lousewort are recognized. The plants, as one variety or another, occur in the two western Canadian provinces, south to New Mexico and west to the mountains of Oregon, Washington, and California, where it is uncommon.

———————

Above: The bracted lousewort is shown with a medley of alpine plants (not all easy to make out). These include shooting stars (*Dodecatheon jeffreyi*), rosy paintbrush (*Castilleja rhexifolia*), pink mountain heather (*Phyllodoce empetriformis*), bistort (*Bistorta bistortoides*), and elephant head lousewort (*Pedicularis groenlandica*)—all described in this book.

### Lewis's monkey-flower
### *Mimulus lewisii* Pursh

Lewis's (also purple) monkey-flower, has large, bright pink to almost purple blooms accentuated by a red-spotted yellow palate on the central petal of the lower lip. Its species name honors Captain Meriwether Lewis who was the first to collect the plant on or near Lemhi Pass on the border of today's Montana and Idaho, in August, 1805 (it still grows there today). Lewis's monkey flower is common in the mountains of Idaho and in all of the surrounding states, in California, and in the two western-most Canadian provinces. It grows along mountain streams and in seep-springs, blooming at least as high as treeline. The flowers are shed whole and float into back waters, often turning the surface pink with floating blooms.

### Subalpine monkey-flower
### *Mimulus tilingii* Regel

The subalpine monkey-flower spreads by shallow roots ("rhizomes") and grows near water at high elevations. Its flowers have a lower "lip" made up of conjoined petals and a furry, variably red-spotted "palate." The plant grows from New Mexico, west to the coastal ranges of the United States and Canada. Heinrich Sylvester Theodor Tiling (1818-1871), a physician-botanist with the Russian American company, collected the plant's seeds near Nevada City, California, in 1868. The flowers of the common yellow mimulus, *Mimulus guttatus* DC. (not shown) look so much like those of this plant that the two species are hard to tell apart (although genetically separate). The yellow mimulus is a taller plant that does not grow at high elevations. It thrives where there is moisture, and has been introduced far from its native west, in North America, and elsewhere as well. Meriwether Lewis found the yellow mimulus near present-day Missoula, Montana, on July 4, 1806.

**Dwarf purple mimulus, *Mimulus nanus* Hook. & Arn.**
The dwarf monkey-flower is a foothill plant found in the Northwest, and in Nevada and California. Its striking little flowers have variable and distinctive dark markings. The plants may grow in such numbers as to turn the ground purple.

**Musk-flower, *Mimulus moschatus* Douglas ex Lindl.**
The musk-flower, named for its odor, is a plant of the Northwest (although, interestingly, a disjunct population grows on the northeastern seaboard, north to Labrador). Four varieties are recognized, although var. *moschatus* shown here is the only one native to Idaho's mountains. The plants usually grow near streams or in other moist places. Because the flowers are obscurely lipped, and the petals have no red markings, the plants may not be recognized as monkey-flowers when first seen.

**Primrose monkey-flower, *Mimulus primuloides* Benth.**
The flowers of the primrose monkey-flower are less than 1/4 of an inch in diameter with crimson-spotted, notched petals. This montane to subalpine plant spreads by rhizomes (shallow roots) to form spreading, dense mats on wet ground. It is native to all of the far western states.

**Downy monkey-flower, *Mimetanthe pilosa* (Benth.) Greene**
The downy, or false, monkey-flower is the only species of *Mimetanthe* (the term means, approximately, "mimulus-like flower") and clearly it is closely related. The plant is tiny. Its flowers, greatly magnified here, measure only about 1/8 inch across. The species name, *pilosa* means "hairy." The downy monkey-flower grows as high as the montane zone throughout the Far West and into Baja, Mexico.

### Blue-eyed Mary
#### *Collinsia parviflora* Douglas ex Lindl. (above, left and right)

Blue-eyed Mary flowers are no more than 1/8 inch long. They are common throughout the West, appearing as tiny blue dots underfoot soon after the snow melts. With magnification, you'll see that the flowers are attractive, with a lower lip made up of two turned-down, blue-tipped white petals. An unclassified form (left above), photographed on the Clearwater River with flowers 1/2 inch long, is sometimes seen in north-central Idaho. It seems to occupy a niche midway between the common blue-eyed Mary (above right) and an even larger species with flowers to 3/4 inch long, *Collinsia grandiflora* Lindl., that grows in the Columbia Gorge, and a plant that Lewis and Clark collected on April 17, 1806, early on their return journey.

### Tweedy's snowlover (left, left center)
#### *Chionophila tweedyi*
#### (Canby  & Rose) L.F. Hend.

Tweedy's snowlover appears soon after the snowmelt. Half a dozen or so lavender-tinged flowers, their lips turned up at the end, bloom on one side of a stem that arises from a basal rosette of small oval leaves. The plant is related to the penstemons, and was formerly classified as *Penstemon tweedyi*. It is found  near treeline in the mountains of Idaho and neighboring Montana. The name honors Frank Tweedy (1854-1937), a topographical engineer with the U.S. Geological Survey. *Chionophila* is from the Greek *xioni* meaning "snow" and *filos* for "friend." The inelegant name "toothbrush flower" has also been applied to the plant.

### Taper-leaf penstemon
### *Penstemon attenuatus* Douglas ex Lindl.

The taper-leaf penstemon (also "sulphur penstemon" for the color of one of its several varieties) is commonly seen in our mountains, sometimes in large numbers. It is characterized by its discrete, crowded flower clusters ("verticillasters") and is sometimes confused with *Penstemon rydbergii* A. Nelson, a similar plant with well defined flower clusters, that grows at lower elevations. Four varieties of taper-leaf penstemon are recognized; all are found in Idaho (we believe this is var. *militaris* [Greene] Cronquist). The species is found mostly in the Northwest, although one variety also occurs in Wyoming.

### Pale yellow penstemon
### *Penstemon confertus* Douglas ex Lindl.

The pale yellow penstemon is found in the northern half of Idaho, British Columbia, Alberta, Oregon and Montana. Its pale yellowish-white ("ochroleucous") flowers distinguish the plant, as do its purple anther sacs and "bearded" stamen. The name *confertus* means "crowded," presumably for the flower clusters, although they are no more crowded than those of many other species. Penstemons may hybridize. This plant, for example, may cross with *Penstemon procerus* and produce a pink-flowered plant. The tendency for penstemons to hybridize suggests to botanists that the genus is actively evolving.

### Dark blue penstemon
### *Penstemon cyaneus* Pennell

The large-flowered, dark blue penstemon is a colorful plant that grows only in Idaho, Montana and Wyoming. A tendency for its flowers to be borne along one side of the stem distinguishes it from the very similar Payette penstemon, *Penstemon payettensis* Nelson & J. F. MacBride, a tall, showy species that grows with sagebrush in central Idaho and adjacent Oregon.

### Twin-leaved penstemon
### *Penstemon diphyllus* Rydb.

The twin-leaved (*"diphyllus"*) penstemon is characterized by large pale-purple flowers whose upper lips are split for more than half their length, and by paired, toothed leaves ranged along the stem. A mountain plant, it grows in southern Idaho, as well as in Washington and Montana.

### Hot-rock penstemon
### *Penstemon deustus* Douglas ex Lindl.

The hot-rock penstemon grows mostly on cliffs and other rocky surfaces. That, as well as its white flowers and shallowly serrated leaves, serves to identify the plant. It is native to all of the northwestern states, Nevada and California. Several varieties are recognized; ours is var. *deustus.*

### Fuzzy-tongue penstemon
### *Penstemon eriantherus* Pursh

The fuzzy-tongue penstemon bears a few large, wide, light-purple flowers with prominent "guide-lines" within the throat. While *eriantherus* means "hairy-anther," the degree of hairiness varies considerably among the five recognized varieties. The Idaho variety, var. *redactus* Pennell & D. D. Keck, is a low plant with a rather sparsely bearded yellow stamen.

### Small-flowered penstemon
### *Penstemon procerus* Douglas ex Graham

This is the most common of Idaho's penstemons. It has small, narrow-tubed, densely arrayed flowers with lips that often close the mouth of the flower. The plants are common throughout the West, from foothills to above tree-line. Several varieties are recognized; ours is var. *procerus.*

### Wilcox's penstemon
### *Penstemon wilcoxii* Rydb.

Wilcox's penstemon grows in the northern half of Idaho, spilling over into neighboring states. The plants are tall, with finely serrated, large stem leaves, and a series of long paired stemlets that bear clusters ("panicles") of moderately large, blue flowers. The plant was found by Meriwether Lewis near Kamiah, Idaho, in 1806.

### Shrubby penstemon
### *Penstemon fruticosus*
### (Pursh) Greene

The shrubby penstemon is an attractive, and common species found in the four northwestern states, in British Columbia and in Wyoming, growing from mid–elevations into the subalpine zone. Its stems are woody, and its leathery leaves are evergreen. When mature, the plants form shrubs that may grow to be quite large. Showy, light-purple flowers are up to two inches long. Several varieties are recognized, identified mostly by the form of the leaves. Ours, illustrated here, with lanceolate, smooth-edged leaves is var. *fruticosus,* the most common variety. Lewis and Clark found the shrubby penstemon while on the Lolo Trail (June 15, 1806).

### Mountain penstemon
### *Penstemon montanus* Greene var.
### *montanus*

This lovely penstemon is another woody species that grows in the mountains of Idaho, Montana, Wyoming and Utah. It is usually encountered by hikers, growing near treeline or higher. Like the shrubby penstemon, it forms well demarcated shrubby clumps. Large violet flowers, woody stems, toothed leaves, and the high elevation at which it grows, serve to identify the plant. A related variety, *Penstemon montanus* var. *idahoensis* (D. D. Keck) Cronquist, with mostly smooth-edged leaves, grows only in Idaho.

217

### American brooklime
### *Veronica americana*\*
### Schwein. ex Benth.

Veronica flowers are irregular. The upper petal is large while the remaining four are distinctly smaller in size. While veronicas in general prefer moist places, some, like the American brooklime, are water plants that grow along the edges of small streams with their roots submerged. (The term "brooklime" was derived from the Middle English "brok-lemok," for a closely related plant. [OED]) Ours is easily identified by its growth preference, by its ovoid, finely serrated leaves and by its small, slightly irregular, blue flowers. The plant is found throughout the United States, except for several southern states. Several other species are also common in Idaho—two more are shown here.

### Cusick's speedwell
### *Veronica cusickii* A. Gray

Cusick's speedwell is a sub-alpine plant that grows in the Pacific coastal states and in Idaho and Montana. Its small flowers are deep blue to violet, borne in a loose terminal cluster, or "raceme." It may be identified by its long, yellow-tipped stamens, and even longer stigmas. William Conklin Cusick (1842-1922) for whom this plant is named taught and ranched in Oregon. He found this namesake plant in the Blue Mountains of Oregon. It was described in 1878 by Harvard's professor of botany, Asa Gray, who classified many new plants sent to him from all over the world. The name "speedwell' has been in use for more than four centuries; it presumably is a testimonial to the plant's perceived medicinal value.

---

\* The name "veronica" has been used for plants in this genus since at least the 1500s, although why they were so named is not known. The original veronica (*vera icon*, the true icon), preserved in St. Peter's in Rome, is the kerchief that a young woman (St. Veronica) used to wipe Christ's face on the road to Calvary. An impression of His face remained on the cloth.

### American alpine speedwell
### *Veronica wormskjoldii*
### Roem. & J. A. Schultes

The American alpine speedwell, *Veronica wormskjoldii*, is an attractive, small sub-alpine flower, found in the mountains of the West, and across the northern part of the continent to Greenland. Its stem is hairy and its flower lack the long anthers and stigmas of Cusick's speedwell shown on the preceding page. Morten Wormskjold (1783-1845) was a Danish botanist who, in 1813, led an expedition to Greenland where he collected many plants, including this one. Later, he accompanied the Kotzebue expedition to the North Pacific in the company of botanists Adelbert von Chamisso and Johann Friedrick Gustav von Eschscholtz; both are mentioned elsewhere in this book.

### Mountain kittentoes
### *Synthyris missurica* (Raf.) Pennel

Mountain kittentoes favor shaded, moist woods. Their tiny four-petaled flowers are similar to those of the veronicas and, for a time, the plant was classified as *Veronica missurica* (with ongoing taxonomic study, it may become so again). The small leafy bracts below the flower cluster help to identify this and several related species, as do its broad, scalloped basal leaves. This species is found only in the Northwest and in California. The plant shown here was photographed in deep woods along US Highway 12 adjacent to the Clearwater River, close to where Meriwether Lewis collected the plant on the expedition's return journey (June 26, 1806).

### Butter-and-egg plant
### *Linaria vulgaris* Hill (above)
### Dalmatian toadflax
### *Linaria dalmatica* (L.) Mill. (center)

When one first sees the common "butter-and-egg plant," its clustered butter-yellow and egg-yolk-orange flowers immediately identify the plant. The butter-and-egg plant and the related Dalmatian toadflax, *Linaria dalmatica* (center) are similiar both in appearance and behavior. The  plants were introduced from Europe as ornamentals during the 1800s, with no concern about the effect that they might have on our native flora. Both grow in Idaho as high as the subalpine zone, sometimes forming dense spreading patches that crowd out other plants. Both species are ranked as serious weeds and both grow throughout the United States.

The two species do differ a bit. The Dalmatian toadflax has a looser flower cluster, the flowers' basal spurs are sharper, the leaves are wider and they clasp the stem—the latter is the most consistent identifying feature. Toadflaxes in general have three-petaled upper and two petaled lower "lips" that meet to resemble a toad's mouth. This and flax-like leaves explain the name "toadflax." *Linaria,* was derived in part from *Linum,* the generic name for flax.

### Common mullein
### *Verbascum thapsus* L. (below)

Because of the taxonomic changes noted in the introduction to this chapter, the common mullein, *Verbascum thapsus* is the only  true Scrophulariaceae shown on these pages. The plant—a serious weed—has spread far and wide since it was introduced from Eurasia and is at home in every state and most Canadian provinces. It grows on dry disturbed ground, alongside roads, in pasture land, near construction sites, and often away from settled places in our mountains. Large dusty-green leaves, long stems,  and dense clusters of irregular, yellow, five-petaled flowers make the common mullein recognizable immediately. The plants are biennial, forming small furry-leaved rosettes the first year, and the familiar long-stalked plants the next. They produce large numbers of hardy seeds—seeds a century old are said to have germinated. Formerly, the plant's leaves were used medicinally for tea, for poultices, and  smoked to treat asthma. Dried mullein stalks, saturated with grease or wax, were used as torches. *Verbascum* is an ancient name for common mulleins; the word mullein is from the Latin *mollis,* meaning "soft," for the velvety leaves, and *Thapsus* is the name of a city in Sicily.

# Nightshade Family (Solanaceae)

The Solanaceae, or Nightshade family is made up of 98 genera and 2,715 species. It includes some of our most important food plants: potatoes, peppers, tomatoes, eggplant, etc. Tobacco plants are also in the nightshade family. Others members contain poisonous alkaloids including atropine-related substances, some of which are therapeutically important: for example, atropine (belladonna), scopolamine, hyosciamine, and other congeners. Various Solanaceae are also favorite ornamentals, including petunias, Japanese lanterns, etc.

While three dozen or so genera are found in North America—mostly as semi-tropical plants—only a few native Solanaceae grow in Idaho. These include species of *Datura* (Jimson-weeds), *Nicotiana* (tobacco plants), and *Physalis* (ground-cherries); none of these are found in our mountains so far as we are aware.

The two plants shown here are included for they grow in our mountains at least as high as the montane zone. Both are common Eurasian imports now at home throughout North America.

The family takes its name from *solanum*, an old Latin name used by Pliny, that means "comforter," probably from the same root as "solace," and reflects the sedative effects of various alkaloidal substances found in this family.

# Solanaceae

## Black henbane
### *Hyoscyamus niger* L.

Black henbane, given its striking appearance, is recognizeable at first glance. An Old World plant, it is now widespread, and because it is toxic to livestock, the plant is considered a noxious weed in Idaho and in several other states. Henbanes contain generous amount of the alkaloid hyoscine (scopolamine) used for millennia as a sedative, and for its atropine-like properties. Scopolamine has been used in obstetrics to induce "twilight sleep," as an adjunct to anesthesia, and—reputedly—for extracting confessions.

## Climbing nightshade,
### *Solanum dulcamara* L.

The climbing nightshade usually grows on disturbed ground. While it is considered a weed, it is not a particularly agressive one. The flowers' reflexed deep purple petals and joined beak-like yellow anthers serve to identify the plant. Although the leaves and unripe fruit are poisonous, its ripe red berries are said to be toxic only if eaten in large quantities. The berries are bitter at first, but then leave a sweet taste explaining the species name, *dulcamara*, Latin for "bittersweet."

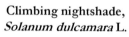

## Valerian Family (Valerianaceae)

The word "valerian" possibly was derived from the Latin word *valere* meaning to be strong, or healthy—a tribute to the plants' supposed medicinal worth. The word has been in use for a long time; the OED's first citation is to Chaucer, who mentioned the plant ca. 1386, and presumably it was named even earlier. The family is not a large one, for it includes only about nine genera and 400 species. While most grow in the north temperate zone, a few are found in the South American Andes. The common European garden heliotrope, *Valeriana officinalis* L. (its species name implies "of the apothecary shop"), resembles the Sitka valerian, a plant common in Idaho's mountains. The roots of the European plant contain a pharmacologically active principle, valerianic acid, said to act as a sedative and sleep aid; presumably the same substance occurs in our plants. Valerian flowers are small, mostly white, clustered, with five petals and three stamens. There are usually paired opposing leaves below the inflorescence. Toward the base, the leaves are whorled, and often compound. Plants belonging to three different genera of Valerianaceae grow in the Northwest, but the four species of genus *Valeriana* shown here are the only members of the family that we have seen in our mountains.

### Edible valerian
### *Valeriana edulis* Nutt. ex Torr. & A. Gray var. *edulis*

The edible valerian, or tobacco root, is a conspicuously leafy plant with several crowded creamy-white flower clusters on each of several thick stems. The species name, *edulis,* means "edible" referring to the plants' bulky roots. Although these were gathered, eaten, and apparently enjoyed by Native Americans, they are, by report, "the most horrid food ever ingested." (Harrington, HD, *Edible Native Plants of the Rocky Mountains*, Univ. New Mexico Press, 1967, p. 223-7). Valerian roots—from which the medically active compound valerianic acid is extracted—have a strong and rather unpleasant odor which some have compared to smelly socks. Cats are attracted to the dried roots: they are said to have the same effect as catnip. Another variety *Valeriana edulis* var. *ciliata* (Torr. & Gray) Cronquist, grows in several mid-western states north to Canada, but ours (var. *edulis*) is found only in the western mountain states to northern Mexico. The plant was found by Thomas Nuttall near today's Walla Walla, Washington.

### Sitka valerian
### *Valeriana sitchensis* Bong.

The Sitka valerian, or mountain heliotrope, common in Idaho, is often found growing in the moist open shade of evergreen forests. The plants bloom in late spring at montane elevations, and later in the subalpine zone. Usually one cluster of small white flowers is borne on each stem. Groups of opposing lanceolate leaves appear at intervals along the stem, growing so closely together as to appear whorled. The leaves are pinnately compound at the base, usually with five leaflets. The plants spread by their roots, so several are often found growing together in one place. Three stamens and a pistil extend well beyond the flowers' five petals, giving the flower head a feathery look. The species name, *sitchensis*, refers to the Russian settlement of Sitka, on Baranof Island, where the plant was first collected by Karl Heinrich Mertens (1796-1830) while on a Russian round-the-world journey (1836-1839).

### Sharp-leaf valerian
### *Valeriana acutiloba* Rydb.
### var. *pubicarpa* (Rydb.) Cronquist

The sharp-leaf valerian has softly bristled seeds, explaining another common name, "downy-fruited valerian." The name *acutiloba* refers to the plants' pointed leaves, the lower ones made up of three large leaflets. It grows as high as treeline in the mountains of all of the western states, blooming early in the summer while north-facing slopes are still snow covered. The small, sometimes pink-tinged, flowers bloom centripetally, as do those in the vervain family (Verbenaceae) explaining another common name, "mountain verbena." The name "cordilleran valerian" has also been suggested as a standardized common name for this plant.

### Northern valerian
### *Valeriana dioica* L. var. *sylvatica*
### (Richardson) S. Watson

The northern, or marsh, valerian, is—like most members of the genus—stout-stemmed. It is a low plant, usually found growing in moist mountain meadows, or on ground wet from the recent snow-melt, at mid- to subalpine elevations. The species name, *dioica*, from the Greek, means "two houses," signifying that there are both male and female plants. While not showy, these are not unattractive plants and are said to do well in wild-flower gardens. The northern valerian is at home in the mountains of most of our western states and Canadian provinces. Because it is a circumboreal species, our plant is classified as var. *sylvatica*, to distinguish it from the slightly different Eurasian variety, var. *dioica*.

## Violet Family (Violaceae)

Violets, wild and cultivated, have been treasured for millennia. (African violets, *Saintpaulia* spp., are not in the violet family at all, but are members of another family, Gesneriaceae.) The family, Violaceae, is made up of 23 genera and 900 species. It is widely distributed; most are found in the north temperate zone. About sixty species are native to the United States, and about half a dozen species grow in our mountains. The name "violet" was derived from the Latin word *viola*, used for a sweet smelling flower, possibly the European violet, *Viola odorata* L., a small pansy-like flower known to Europeans as "hearts-ease," and to us as "Johnny-jump-up"; the plant is believed to be an ancestor of today's cultivated pansies.

Violets typically have five sepals and five separated petals. The flowers are irregular but bilaterally symmetrical, with a large, sometimes bearded lower petal. A nectar-containing sac or spur attached to the lower petal may extend backward behind the flower. Most violets prefer shade and moisture, but some, like our upland yellow violet, *Viola praemorsa*, flourish on dry ground. Violets tend to be spring bloomers, recognizing that "spring" for flowers represents a condition rather than a date, and varies with altitude. Some species may flower again in the fall if the weather is mild.

The family has little economic importance beyond its many popular pansy cultivars.

**Hooked violet**
***Viola adunca* Sm.**

If, in hiking along our muddy trails and through spring-moist meadows, you see blue violets, they are most likely *Viola adunca* the hooked violet, (also early blue violet). Look closely at the flower and you will see that it has an upward turned spur, derived from part of the lower central petal. The hooked violet grows throughout the West and across northern North America. Our plant is var. *adunca;* two other varieties grow only in California. The name, *adunca,* means "hook" in Latin.

**Upland yellow violet**
***Viola praemorsa* Douglas ex Lindl.**
**var. *linguifolia* M.S. Baker**
**& J. C. Clausen ex M. E. Peck**

The plant shown here, known locally and in our first edition, as the goosefoot violet, *Viola purpurea,* is a variety of the upland yellow violet. It is commonly seen growing on gravelly slopes, often in the company of sagebrush. The plant is one of the earliest flowers to bloom in the spring, appearing immediately after snow-melt at ever higher elevations as high as the subalpine zone. *Viola praemorsa* grows in the coastal states from Oregon to California, east to Wyoming, Utah and Colorado. It is also found, rarely, in British Columbia and Alberta.

### Small white violet
### *Viola macloskeyi* F. E. Lloyd

The common name "small white violet" suits this plant, for its purple-marked flowers are the smallest of any of our violets. The plants grow from mid-elevations to high in our mountains. The little flowers are hard to photograph for they are often tangled up in a mat of variable, kidney and heart-shaped leaves. Macloskey's violet is widely distributed. It occurs along both coasts, in our northern states and in the Canadian provinces (although rare in Alberta and Saskatchewan). Two varieties are recognized, one with scalloped leaves, var. *pallens* (Hanks ex Ging.) C.L. Hitch., and the other with smooth-edged leaves, var. *macloskeyi*. The latter is said not to occur in Idaho, although those shown here fit the description of that variety. George Macloskey (1834-1920), for whom the species was named, was born in Ireland. He held degrees in both theology and in natural sciences, becoming professor of biology at Princeton University in 1874, a chair he held until 1906.

### Valley violet
### *Viola vallicola* A. Nelson

Previously known, incorrectly, as Nuttall's violet (a plant confined to the Great Plains), the valley violet is distinguished by its large lanceolate leaves. These may be smooth-edged, or have shallow teeth as in the illustration. The plant grows throughout the West in both the United States and Canada, ranging as far east as Kansas and the Dakotas. It grows from mid- to high elevations along stream banks and on moist ground. Thomas Nuttall (1786-1839) was a British botanist who worked in the United States during the early decades of the 19th century. The excellence of his work gained him a position on the faculty of Harvard College. He botanized widely throughout what is now the United States, explaining why his name is attached to such a variety of plants (and birds). Nuttall returned to an ancestral home in England in later life.

### Pioneer violet
### *Viola glabella* Nutt.

The pioneer, or stream violet grows in northern California, throughout the Northwest, north to Alaska and in eastern Asia. It appears in great numbers in northern Idaho, preferring the moist ground of deep woods and streambanks. It may be identified by its bright yellow flowers marked with black pencilling, and by its heart- or kidney-shaped leaves. The plant was collected first by Thomas Nuttall in the coastal mountains of Oregon in the spring of 1835.

# Iris Family (Iridaceae)

The Iridaceae, a family with many colorful flowers, is appropriately named for Iris, the Greek goddess of the rainbow. The family is made up of sixty genera and 1,845 species world-wide. Many Iridaceae—*Gladiolus*, *Crocus*, *Freesia*, *Iris*, and others—are found wherever flowers are cultivated; ornamental plants are the family's main economic importance. Most are perennials, spreading by bulbs and root-like stems ("rhizomes") and by seeds. A non-botanist looking at an iris's showy flower may have difficulty identifying the parts, but usually there are three bent back petal-like sepals ("falls"), and three erect petals ("standards") joined at their base to form a swollen floral tube—a family characteristic. There are three hidden stamens and three stigmas which—confusingly—in some species take the shape and color of a petal. Leaves are "equitant," meaning that the sides of the longitudinally folded leaves ride on either side of adjacent stems. The parallel-veined leaves are otherwise typical of monocotyledonous plants in general. Only three wild irises are found in Idaho. One, not shown here, is *Iris versicolor*, the harlequin iris, common in the northeastern states and provinces. A disjunct population—it is a rare plant in Idaho—grows at the head of Priest Lake in Idaho's panhandle. The other two, the western blue flag (*Iris missouriensis)* and the yellow flag (*Iris pseudoacora*—an import), are shown on the following page in company with another member of the family, our native blue-eyed grass, *Sisyrhinchium idahoense.*

### Western blue flag
### *Iris missouriensis* Nutt.

The western blue flag grows in many western states. It is easily identified, for it looks like a garden iris on a diet, blooming in late spring to mid-elevations on the banks of slow flowing streams and in moist meadows. Its color varies from light to dark blue according to location. Meriwether Lewis collected the plant while ascending the Blackfoot River in Montana on his return trip (July 5th, 1806). Only fragments of the plant survived, so botanist Frederick Pursh could not publish a description. It was again found by Nathaniel Wyeth in 1833 and described by his friend, Thomas Nuttall. Not everyone is enchanted by this attractive plant; it is classified as a weed in California and Nevada.

### Yellow flag
### *Iris pseudacorus* L.

The yellow flag was imported from the Old World as an ornamental water plant. It has made itself at home in the New World, forming spreading clumps in the shallow water of ponds and streams (the plant shown was photographed in Blaine County's Silver Creek, prime trout water). It is immediately identifiable by its pale to deep-yellow flowers and its growth habit. The yellow flag is also classified as a noxious weed in Nevada and California.

### Idaho blue-eyed grass
### *Sisyrhinchium idahoense* E. P. Bricknell
### var. *occidentale* (E. P. Bricknell) D. M. Hend.

The blue-eyed grasses are Iridaceae, with narrow, grass-like basal leaves. A single flower on the end of a naked stem bears three blue petaloid sepals and three matching petals with pointed tips. In the past many sisyrinchiums were lumped into one species, more recently they have been split into many. Blue-eyed grasses favor moist meadows and are said to do well in ornamental gardens. The name *Sisyrhinchus* was used by Greek natural historian Theophrastus (372-287 BC) for an iris-like plant.

# Lily Family (Liliaceae)

The lily family (including many newly recognized, related families), consists of almost 300 genera and 5,000 species. It has always been considered a taxonomic catch-all family, one made up of many diverse genera with a few common characteristics. While most have bulbs or "corms" (thick bulb-like stems) that divide below ground, some spread by rhizomes (creeping underground stems). All have the parallel-veined leaves, characteristic of monocotyledonous plants in general. Most also are perennial, herbaceous (non-woody) plants whose flowers have three sepals and three petals (often modified into six identical "tepals"). Despite these common features, there is good reason—based on morphologic and molecular differences—to divide the Liliaceae into a number of smaller families. There is less agreement among taxonomists, however, as to how this should be done.

It seems reasonable, at least for our purposes, to retain the older classification while indicating those new families that are now generally accepted. These include:

Agavaceae (Agave family), *Camassia*

Alliaceae (Onion family), *Allium*

Calochortaceae (Mariposa lily family) *Calochortus*

Liliaceae (Lily family) *Clintonia, Prosartes* (formerly *Disporum)*,
    *Erythronium, Fritillaria, Lloydia*, and *Streptopus*

Melanthaceae (Bunchflower family), *Trillium, Stenanthium, Veratrum,*
        *Xerophyllum, Toxicoscordion* and *Anticlea* (the last two genera were
        until recently assigned to a broadly defined species, *Zigadenus).*

Ruscaceae (Butcher's broom family), *Maianthemum*

Themidaceae (Cluster lily family), *Triteleia*

# Liliaceae (Agavaceae)

## Common camas
### *Camassia quamash* (Pursh) Greene

The Indian word *quamash* is the source of both generic and species names for this plant; it also supplied the common name, anglicized as "camas." Explorers were amazed when they saw fields of camas in bloom. Meriwether Lewis, wrote, in June of 1806, that the plants stretched like "lakes of fine clear water."

In Idaho and adjacent states, the flowers still form spectacular "lakes" each spring on water-soaked fields. Their bulbs are the size of a small onion and are palatable both raw and cooked. They store well across the seasons making them a prime food source for Native Americans. The members of the Lewis and Clark expedition gratefully ate camas roots in the camp of Nez Perce Indians following the perilous crossing of the Bitterroot Mountains in the autumn of 1805. Many of the explorers became sick. Meriwether Lewis almost died, blaming the roots for his illness (more likely their gastroenteritis was derived from tainted salmon that the Indians gave them). Nevertheless, he gathered a specimen of camas on the Weippe Prairie, in June of 1806, while waiting to cross the Lolo Trail on the return journey. The distinctive flowers are large with six identical tepals and bright yellow parenthesis-shaped anthers. Flower color ranges considerably from one location to another, from almost white, to shades of blue, to the blue-gray color shown here, to purple. The illustration below shows a "lake" on Camas Prairie near Fairfield, one of several "Camas Prairies" in Idaho.

### Hooker's onion
### *Allium acuminatum* Hook.

Hooker's onion (also taper-tip onion) was collected by Archibald Menzies, ship's surgeon and botanist of the Vancouver Expedition, on today's Vancouver Island in the 1790s. It was later classified by William Jackson Hooker, then professor of botany in Glasgow, and later director of England's Kew Gardens. His name is still associated with the plant. The word "acuminate" means "to taper to a sharp point," from the shape of the tepals. Each of our wild onions has its own ecological niche. This one prefers dry ground, growing to moderately high elevations and blooming in summer after other flowers have gone by. Said to be the commonest wild onion in the Northwest, it is found throughout the mountain West. The pink to purple flowers are borne in a loose umbel atop a long, thin, leafless stem. The leaves are rather wispy and inconspicuous, and have usually dried up by the time the flowers appear.

### Short-styled onion
### *Allium brevistylum* S. Watson

The short-styled onion (the common name is a translation of the scientific species name) is a tall plant whose flowers are borne in a loose umbel. The flowers do not open widely and the short style, from which the plant takes its names, can't be seen easily, as it can with many other onions. The plant's stems are much longer than its leaves. It prefers streambanks and other moist locations, growing at least as high as treeline. At lower altitudes the leaves are bright green as shown here; at tree-line they take on a reddish hue. The plant grows only in Idaho, Wyoming, Colorado and Utah.

### Brandegee's onion
### *Allium brandegeei* S. Watson

Brandegee's onion grows on gravelly hillsides at all elevations, appearing soon after the snowmelt. Often there are so many as to almost turn the ground white with their flowers. It is a species often seen in our mountains, growing from northeastern Oregon, across southern and central Idaho to Utah. Disjunct populations also occur in neighboring states. Each flower has six tepals and each tepal has a dark rib, often more obvious on the outer side. The flowers, usually white, are occasionally pink. Its leaves and the bulbs taste much like garden onions (*Allium cepa* L.) and were used in the same way by early settlers. Animals also appreciate the plants; the leaves are often cropped—as in the illustration—by grazing deer. The species name refers to Townshend Stith Brandegee (1843-1925), an American civil engineer, botanist and plant collector, who collected the plant in the Elk Mountains of Colorado.

### Geyer's onion
### *Allium geyeri* S. Watson var. *tenerum* M. E. Jones

Geyer's onion is another common Rocky Mountain onion that grows, often in large numbers, along mountain streams and in moist meadows, sometimes in company with the short-style onion shown on the previous page. Two varieties occur in Idaho, var. *geyeri* in which the heads lack small bulbs ("bulbils"), and var. *tenerum* (*tenerum* means "tender," or "soft") in which many, or all of the flowers are replaced by bulbils. A tall white-flowered onion, the bulbils, when present, make identication easy. The species name honors Charles A. Geyer (1809-1853), a German botanist and plant-hunter who was hired to collect plants in the western United States. In 1843 he traveled across "upper Oregon" (today's western Montana, northern Idaho and eastern Washington) gathering thousands of plant specimens; a dozen or so now bear his name.

### Chive
### *Allium schoenoprasum* L.

Wild chives have a rather spotty distribution across the northern states and Canadian provinces, west into Asia and Europe. Our wild plant appears identical to the garden chive (as it should; it is the same species). The plant is easily identified—most everyone knows what chives looks like. Even lacking its light purple flower head, the typical appearance of its hollow leaves and its taste should clinch its identification. The species name, *schoenoprasum*, is derived from two Greek words meaning "rush" and "leek." Strictly, "chive" (an Old English word) should refer to the plant, and "chives" to its culinary use.

### *Allium simillimum* L. F. Hend.

The pink onion shown on the left was photographed on a mountain trail immediately north of the Sun Valley resort. We included this illustration in the first edition of this book as *Allium aase,* a similar, but uncommon pink-flowered species found only in Ada County. Several botanists acquainted with the latter plant disputed the classification. Since, a specimen has been examined by three knowledgeable botanists who believe it to be a form of *Allium simillimum* a (usually) white-tepaled plant found in Idaho and (rarely) in Montana. The name *simillimum,* from the Latin, means "similiar to," possibly to another species of wild onion. There seems to be no established common name for the plant.

### Tolmie's onion
### *Allium tolmiei* Baker

Tolmie's onion is an attractive plant, although not a particularly common one. It is found in the western part of north-central Idaho and in the coastal states from northeastern California to northeastern Washington. The most common variety, shown here, grows throughout that range. Two other localized varieties that differ slightly in morphology are also recognized. Tolmie's onion grows on dry, gravelly ground, rather than in the moist areas preferred by many other members of the family. It may be identified by its pink flowerheads and especially by its leaves. These are notably wide, flat and sickle-shaped and are quite long compared to the short-stemmed flowerheads. The anthers are longer—up to twice as long—as the tepals in this variety.

William Frazer Tolmie (1812-1886) was a surgeon with the Hudson's Bay Company. He was given a plant collection, including this onion, by a friend. Tolmie sent the collection to William Jackson Hooker in England. Subsequently Tolmie's name was attached to the plant. Tolmie explored the country around Mt. Rainier in 1833 and apparently hoped—or possibly even attempted—to climb the mountain. (Later, others attempted the climb, but the first successful ascent was not until 1870.)

### Feathery false Solomon's seal
### *Maianthemum racemosum* (L.) Link
### var. *amplexicaule* (Nutt.) Dorn

The feathery false Solomon's seal (also western false Solomon's plume, and wild lily of the valley) is a common plant found in much of North America. Until recently the two plants shown on this page were in the genus *Smilacina* and are still so identified in many guide books. On the basis of recent studies, however, they have been placed in the butcher's broom family (Ruscaceae) and in the genus *Maianthemum*. (The latter name was derived from two Greek words for "May" and "flower.") The maianthemums, and many similar lily-like plants, commonly grow in forest shade, and in other moist situations. Deep green, parallel-veined leaves, and a spray of small-petaled, yellow-anthered, white flowers make identification easy. Green berries turn red as they ripen. Botanists recognize two varieties; ours, var. *amplexicaule* (the word means "stem-clasping" for the leaves) is a western plant. The other, var. *racemosum*, grows in the east; the two varieties are separated by the Great Plains.

### Starry false Solomon's seal
### *Maianthemum stellatum* (L.) Link

As is common with widely distributed plants, the starry false Solomon's seal has many common names. These include star-flowered (or western) Solomon's plume, wild (or false) lily of the valley and others. The plant is quite similar in appearance to the feathery false Solomon's seal shown above, differing in that its leaves are narrower, its tepals are larger, and the flowers are star-shaped (the species name, *stellata*, is derived from the Latin word *stella* for "star"). The starry false Solomon's seal grows in all of the states and provinces of North America, excepting only Texas and the southern seaboard states.

**Large-flowered triplet-lily**
*Triteleia grandiflora* Lindl.

The large flowered triplet-lily is an attractive flower; now classified in the cluster lily family (Themidaceae). It blooms early in dry meadows to mid elevations. Its flowers have three outer and three inner tepals; the latter have ruffled edges. Flower color ranges from white with blue markings (var. *grandiflora*) to blue with darker lines (var. *howellii* [S. Watson] Hoover). The species grows in the northwestern states, British Columbia, Utah and—uncommonly—in neighboring states.

Originally collected by David Douglas, the plant was until recently classified as a *Brodiaea,* a genus with three-anthered flowers. The British botanist John Lindley (1799-1865), published a description of our plant in 1830, noting that its flowers have six anthers (as Douglas had noted) and placed it in a new genus, *Triteleia.* Recent studies have shown that his classification was correct— although it is still often listed as "Douglas's brodiaea." Meriwether Lewis collected the plant while ascending the Columbia River (April 17, 1806). Frederick Pursh noted that Lewis's flower had six anthers. Unfortunately, he classified it as a *Brodiaea,* so missing a chance to describe and name a new genus.

**Glacier lily**
*Erythronium grandiflorum* Pursh var. *grandiflorum*

Glacier lilies are found through the northwestern states and provinces, and east into the Rocky Mountain states. As with other well-loved and widely distributed plants, this one has many common names: glacier lily, avalanche lily, trout lily, dog-tooth violet, fawn lily, adder's tongue and others. It is a common plant in parts of Idaho. Although we have not seen it growing south of Lemhi Pass (30 miles south-east of Salmon), it grows further south in the mountains of the southeastern part of the state. Lewis and Clark collected the glacier lily near their Kooskooskee (Clearwater) River campsite on May 8, 1806 and later on the Lolo Trail. A related white variety, var. *candidum* Piper, grows only in northern Idaho, Washington and Montana.

### Elegant mariposa lily
### *Calochortus elegans* Pursh var. *elegans*

The elegant mariposa lily's small flower only measures about an inch across. The plant was first collected by Meriwether Lewis on May 17, 1806, near todays Kamiah, Idaho. He brought the dried specimen back to the United States where botanist Frederick Pursh recognized that the plant was new to science. He coined the name *Calochortus* (from two Greek words meaning "beautiful plant") for a new genus giving the plant the scientific name that it has today. There are several varieties of *Calochortus elegans* including var. *nanus* Ownbey (southeastern Oregon and northern California) and var. *selwayensis* Ownbey (Idaho and Montana).

### White mariposa lily
### *Calochortus eurycarpus* S. Watson

The white mariposa lily (also know as the star tulip) is identified by the deep purple spot at the base of each petal. Further in there is a bristle-lined yellow to green "gland." The petals are delta-shaped; the sepals are only a little longer than the petals. The species grows in Idaho and the six surrounding states. Great numbers appear in early to mid-summer in our mountains, growing almost to treeline. The plants are known regionally as "sego lilies," although the true sego lily is *Calochortus nuttallii*, the Utah state flower, occurring farther south. This plant's species name means "broad seed," from the Greek.

### Sagebrush mariposa lily
### *Calochortus macrocarpus* Douglas

The sagebrush mariposa lily (also "green-banded mariposa lily) is a foothill plant that blooms in mid- to late summer on dry sagebrush slopes south of the Clearwater River drainage. The species name means "long fruit" for the shape of the fruit. The three petals and three sepals are the same color, ranging from pale pink to lavender. Its narrow sepals are noticeably longer than the petals; the latter are ovoid with pointed tips. A green band may sometimes may be seen running down the center of each petal (usually more prominent on the back), ending at a rounded basal gland fringed with a border of bright yellow to greenish hairs. Ownbey, in Hitchcock et al., writing about the genus in general, noted that "despite the quantities of bulbs that have been dug in the wild . . . not a single species can be said to have been established in cultivation successfully" (*Vascular Plants of the Pacific Northwest*, 1972). Enjoy these plants where they grow!

### Fairy bells
### *Prosartes trachycarpa* S. Watson

Fairy bells grow in the shade of evergreen forests at higher altitudes, often in the company of species of *Maianthemum* (false Solomon seals), and *Berberis repens* (creeping Oregon grape). The plants are easily identified by their wide, parallel-veined leaves and long-stalked lily-like, paired flowers (above). The ovaries mature into bright red, irregularly shaped berries (below). The berries are said to be edible, but tasteless. Until recently this plant was classified as *Disporum trachycarpum*. Now it has a restored generic name, *Prosartes,* apparently derived from a Greek word meaning "attached," referring to the ovules in the fruit. Our species grows in many western states and Canadian provinces, with disjunct populations in the East.

### Clintonia
### *Clintonia uniflora*
### (Menzies ex Schultes) Kunth

Clintonias go by many common names including beadlily, bluebead lily, bride's bonnet, and queen's cup, and simply "clintonia." They are shade-loving, montane to subalpine plants with a six-tepaled, single white flower (*uniflora*). Their stems arise from a cluster of two or more wide, rather leathery leaves. Each plant bears one blue berry (below). They grow in coastal mountain ranges from California to Alaska, and inland to Idaho and Montana. The name, *Clintonia*, honors amateur naturalist DeWitt Clinton (1769-1828), also known for his political career as a senator, presidential candidate, promoter of steam navigation, and governor of New York.

## Yellow bell
### *Fritillaria pudica*
### (Pursh) Spreng. (left, right)

Yellow-bells (also yellow fritillaries, and yellow mission-bells) bloom in April at lower elevations and well into June higher up, as single plants or in small groups. Narrow, twisted leaves appear first, followed by the flowers. These have six tepals arranged in two rows. Its tepals are yellow-orange with a deep red basal band. The plant is native to most of the far western states. Its species name, *pudica*, means "modest," for the shy, downward facing flowers. *Fritillaria*, in turn, was derived from a Latin word for "dicebox," presumably for the seed-containing capsule (right). Lewis and Clark collected the plant on the Clearwater River (May 8, 1806).

## Checker lily (left)
### *Fritillaria affinis* (Schultes) Sealy
## Chocolate lily (right)
### *Fritillaria atropurpurea* Nutt.

These two plants are clearly related, although their ranges differ. Both bloom about a month later than the yellow-bell shown above. The chocolate lily grows in the southern half of Idaho, and in states to the south. The checker lily grows farther north in Idaho and in the northwestern states to British Columbia. Neither plant is particularly common and finding one is a cause for comment. Fritillaries are sometimes called "rice-roots" for a myriad of tiny bulblets attached to a main bulb. Lewis and Clark collected *Fritillaria affinis* while ascending the Columbia River (April 10, 1806).

## Common alpine lily
### *Lloydia serotina* (L.) Reichenb. var. *serotina*

The alp lily (more commonly known simply as "lloydia") is an alpine plant found in the mountains of many of the western states (although rare in Oregon), north to Alaska and in the mountains of Eurasia. It is an unprepossessing little plant, a true alpine species. A few narrow, inconspicuous leaves and yellow-anthered, white, six-tepaled flowers less than a quarter of an inch across, identify the plant as a lloydia. The plant was named for Edward Lloyd (1660-1709), prominent Welsh author, naturalist, and curator of the Ashmolean Library of Oxford University, who discovered this plant growing in Wales and recognized that true alpine flora grew above treeline in the Welsh mountains. The scientific species name, *serotina*, means "late" or "autumnal"; a strange choice, for the flowers bloom while there is snow on surrounding slopes. A rare yellow variety, var. *flava* (Calder & Roy L. Taylor) B. Boivin, occurs in British Columbia.

## Clasping-leaf twisted-stalk
### *Streptopus amplexicaulis* (L.) DC

The twisted-stalk's stem zigzags from one leaf node to the next as reflected in its generic name, *Streptopus* (from the Greek meaning "twisted foot") and its stemless leaves clasp the main stem. Dependent white flowers have reflexed (turned back) tepals. Its oval red berries, confusingly, are described as both edible and poisonous, according to which guide-book one consults. The plants grow at subalpine elevations in our mountains, usually in the deep shade of evergreen forests. Twisted stalks are found in most of the western states and across the northern part of the continent.

### Western stenanthium
### *Stenanthium occidentale* A. Gray (left)

The western stenanthium grows along stream banks, and in moist meadows. It is the only *Stenanthium* native to the West (another species is found in the eastern United States). Ours occurs in northern California, British Columbia, Alberta and in the four northwestern states; we have seen it growing only in the northern part of Idaho. Dainty, nodding, bronze-colored, lily-like flowers with six recurved tepals are borne on downward-curving stemlets that come off at intervals along a slender stem. Several moderately wide leaves surround the base. *Stenanthium* is derived from two Greek words meaning "narrow flower," apparently for their small size. The common name, "western featherbells" has been suggested for the plant.

### Western trillium (below)
### *Trillium ovatum* Pursh

The western trillium is a spring flower that often blooms while surrounded by banks of snow. The name "*ovatum*" refers to its pointed, oval leaves. Its three-petaled flowers are white, turning pink and then a light purple as they mature (below). Trillium flowers vary in size; tending to be smaller at higher elevations. We have not seen trilliums growing south of the Clearwater River drainage. Meriwether Lewis collected the western trillium on the Columbia River below today's The Dalles, on April 10, 1806. The western trillium is found in all of the Pacific coastal states and British Columbia, east to Montana, and—rarely—in the neighboring Rocky Mountain states.

On June 15, 1806, while on the Lolo Trail, Lewis and Clark collected *Trillium petiolatum* Pursh (the purple trillium, not shown), It is an uncommon species, characterized by a reddish-purple three- petaled flowers and long-stemmed round leaves. The plant is found the northern half of Idaho and in Washington and Oregon.

**California false hellebore**
***Veratrum californicum* Dur.**

California false hellebores (also corn-lilies, from their large leaves and budding flowers) are usually known simply as "veratrums." They appear in late spring growing on moist ground as high as treeline. Lewis and Clark collected the plant along the Lolo Trail in northern Idaho on June 25, 1806, but as it was not flowering it could not be classified. The Greek *elleboros*, and Latin *veratrum* were used in antiquity for poisonous plants. Later, veratrums were given the Latin name *Veratrum* and plants in the buttercup family became *Helleborus*. Plants in both genera are poisonous. The poisons are pharmacologically active—*Helleborus* species contain cardiac glycosides, and veratrum extract was used to treat hypertension. *Veratrum californicum* occurs in all of the western mountain and coastal states. Another variety, var. *caudatum* (A. Heller) C. L. Hitchc. also grows in Idaho. The two varieties are so similar that either will be recognized immediately as a California false hellebore.

## Liliaceae  (Melanthaceae)

**Bear grass**
*Xerophyllum tenax*
**(Pursh) Nutt.**

Bear grass (also Indian basket grass) is one of the Northwest's more spectacular plants. A basal tuft of leaves (the "grass") forms during snowmelt. A few weeks later, a tall stalk tipped with myriad little lily-like blooms appears. The leaves are ideally suited for basket making for they are strong, hard, and even in width almost to their tips. Lewis and Clark saw baskets woven from the grass during the winter of 1805-1806 while at the expedition's Fort Clatsop on the Columbia estuary. Then, the following spring, while in today's Idaho, they saw the plants blooming. Lewis collected two intact blooms during the crossing of the Lolo Trail (June 15, 1806).

Bear grass is found in all of the northwestern states and provinces. We have not seen it in Idaho's mountains south of the southern approach to Lost Trail Pass (US Rt. 93) on the Idaho-Montana border.

## Elegant camus
### *Anticlea elegans* (Pursh) Rydb.

The elegant camas (also mountain death camas, formerly classified as *Zigadenus elegans*) grows, sometimes in great numbers, in mountain meadows as high as treeline. Usually about a foot high, the plants may grow to twice that height in favorable situations. They flower from early to mid-summer, according to elevation. As the name *elegans* suggests, it is the most attractive of our three death camases. Its white flowers are large and the tepals are marked with heart-shaped green "glands" at their bases. All of the death camases are poisonous; this one is said to be least so—also, since it grows at higher elevations it is less accessible to grazing stock. The elegant camas was collected by Meriwether Lewis in the vicinity of today's Lewis and Clark Pass near Lincoln, Montana, on July 7, 1806. Elegant camas is widely distributed, from Alaska south to Mexico in the West, east in Canada to Hudson's Bay and in the United States to the Great Lakes with scattered populations even further to the east.

## Foothill death camas
### *Toxicoscordion paniculatum* (Nutt.) Rydb.

The foothill death camas appears in early spring, and blooms at about the same time as the common camas, usually in early June. A naked stem is topped by a cluster of small, white, six-tepaled flowers. The flowers have six anthers that protrude beyond the tepals, and three styles. Several flowers are borne on each stemlet (botanically, these are panicles, explaining its scientific species name).

The closely related and very similar meadow death camas, *Toxicoscordion venenosum* (S. Watson) Rydb.—the species Latin name means "very poisonous"—has larger, tight-clustered flowers, one flower to each stemlet. Both plants are poisonous and may be lethal to browsing animals, or to humans if they eat the roots. Native Americans were aware of this and harvested the roots of the edible common camas while both plants were in bloom to avoid potentially fatal mistakes—the roots are quite similar to those of the death camases. Until recently the death camases were all classified as species of *Zigadenus* and are still so listed in most guide books. The generic name *Toxicoscordion*, from the Greek, means "poisonous garlic." The plants are found in parts of all of the Rocky Mountain states, and west to the Pacific coastal states.

## Orchid Family (Orchidaceae)

The word "orchid" is derived from the Latin word *orchis*, a term used by Pliny the Elder (23-79 A.D.) in his encyclopedia, *Natural History*, and ultimately from a similar Greek word meaning "testicle" from the shape of the pseudobulb found in many orchid plants. The family consists of 790 genera and some 18,500 species. Given such numbers, it is surprising that the orchid family's only food use is the flavoring derived from Mexican *Vanilla* species. The family's economic importance is derived almost completely from cultivation of its spectacular flowers. Some of its members have made the step from the tropics and sub-tropics to colder environments while evolving progressively less showy flowers. Orchids grow as far north as Siberia, Iceland, Greenland and throughout North America. Many of the tropical orchids are epiphytic (*i.e.*, live on other plants), whereas those in temperate zones are mostly terrestrial. Orchids are usually perennials that spread by underground stems ("rhizomes"), as well as by tiny wind-sown seeds—their seeds are the smallest found in any plant. Species belonging to nine genera occur in Idaho; a few are quite showy. Our wild orchids should never be picked. Their growth requirements are highly selective and often depend on the presence of specific fungal symbionts; they will not survive transplantation.

## Fairy-slipper
### *Calypso bulbosa* (L.) Oakes
### var. *occidentalis* (Holz.) B. Boivin

The fairy-slipper is one of the most colorful of our orchids. It is not a rare plant, but it is elusive, for it favors the floor of evergreen forests where it blooms in late spring. So far as we are aware, it is not found south of the Clearwater River drainage in Idaho. Lewis and Clark—most likely Meriwether Lewis—discovered this then new-to-science plant blooming along the Lolo Trail and collected one as a specimen on June 16, 1806. The plant shown here was photographed in the DeVoto Grove, west of the Lolo Pass, close to where the explorers found theirs. Another variety, var. *americana* (R. Br.) Luer occurs (rarely) in Idaho.

## Spotted coral-root
### *Corallorhiza maculata* (Raf.) Raf.
### var. *occidentalis* (Lindl.) Ames

Coral roots are saprophytes. The flowers shown here—magnified about four times lifesize—are those of a relatively common orchid that grows in moist to fairly dry open shade of forests where its slender, reddish-brown stems stand out. The flowers with their spotted white lips are striking, but you will need a hand lens to see them well, true of many of our native orchids. Another variety, var. *maculata,* also occurs in Idaho. It is a similar plant, with a narrower flower lip. The spotted coral-root is widely distributed across the United States and Canada, occuring in all but a few mid-western and southern states.

### Yellow coral-root
### *Corallorhiza trifida* Châtelaine

Because the coral-roots—named for the bright red color of their root systems—are saprophytes, they lack chlorophyll. Their "leaves" are represented by sheathing bracts seen on the lower part of the stems. The color of coral-roots ranges from the reddish-brown of the spotted coral-root shown on the previous page, to the yellowish color of this plant. This plant's species name, *trifida*, means three-lobed, describing the irregular end of the flower's lip. This plant is also widely distributed all across northern North America, to Alaska, the Arctic Islands and Greenland.

### Western rattlesnake plantain
### *Goodyera oblongifolia* Raf.

The rattlesnake plantain catches the eye only because its several, deep-green, basal leaves are mottled with a central white stripe; it is otherwise a rather plain little plant. Apparently the name "rattlesnake plantain," comes from a fancied resemblance of the leaves' markings (below) to those of rattlesnakes. Whitish flowers (left) form a loose cluster at the top of the plant's stem; then, later in the summer one sees only the basal leaves and a dried stem. Interestingly, because the pedicels (stemlets) are twisted, the plant's flowers are upside-down ("resupinate") and a sepal is fused with two petals to form a "hood." Look for this little orchid in shaded woods. The generic name *Goodyera* honors English botanist, John Goodyer (1592-1664). This orchid is also widely distributed in our West, north to Alaska and with a separate population in eastern Canada.

### White bog orchid
### *Platanthera dilatata*
### (Pursh) Lindl. ex L. C. Beck

As with other widely distributed plants, the white bog orchid has several names: "rein orchid," (for the strap-like lower lip), "boreal orchid," (boreal means "northern") and "habenaria" (the plant's former generic name). There are several varieties, distinguished by slight differences in the flowers. The plant shown here is the most common variety, var. *dilatata.*. It grows in the West from Alaska to the northwestern states and south to Utah and Colorado. In the East, it ranges from Manitoba to Greenland, and south to the northern tier states from Illinois to New England. The plant is often found above treeline. Examine its small white flowers—they are only 1/4" in diameter—but with magnification (top left), you'll see that this is unmistakably an orchid. The flowers, like those of *Goodyera,* are resupinate. A ventral lip, two sepals extending laterally, and a "hood" made up of a dorsal sepal and petals are family characteristics. A prominent downward-curving spur confirms the species' identification. The name *Platanthera*, from the Greek, means "wide (or flat) anther"; *dilatata*, from the Latin means "broad" or "wide," apparently referring to the ventral lip's wide base.

### Slender bog orchid
### *Platanthera stricta* Lindl.

The slender bog orchid (formerly *Habenaria saccata* Greene), while not uncommon, is less often encountered than the plant shown above. As its former classification *saccata* suggests, it is characterized by a swollen, sac-like "scrotiform" spur that hangs down behind the flower. The species name, *stricta*, means "straight." Lindley, who described the plant, apparently used it to refer to the narrow flower cluster. The plant occurs throughout the West, from Alaska to New Mexico.

### Hooded ladies'-tresses
### *Spiranthes romanzoffiana* Cham.

Hooded ladies'-tresses are found all across the North American continent and in most of the northern and western states. (Disjunct populations are even found in the British Isles!) In our area the plant grows as high as the alpine zone. Its stemless flowers are borne on a stout spike-like stem. Each flower is offset a few degrees from the one below, forming the spiral that gives the plant its generic name. The petals (except for the ventral lip) join to form a hood. *Spiranthes* is derived from two Greek words, *speira* meaning "coil" or "spiral" and *anthos* for "flower." The species name honors Nicolai von Romanzov (1734-1826), the Grand Chancellor of the Russian Empire, who sponsored—and funded—the around-the-world expedition led by explorer Otto von Kotzebue (1787-1846) in the years 1815-1818.

### Mountain lady's-slipper
### *Cypripedium montanum* Douglas ex Lindl.

The mountain lady's slipper bears flowers that are smaller and more numerous than those of other species of *Cypripedium*; still, with its showy white blooms it, too, is an elegant plant. Two other lady's slippers are native to Idaho. The one shown here is the most common of the three—finding one will make a hiker's day. Meriwether Lewis encountered the mountain lady's-slipper on the Lolo Trail and again at Traveler's Rest, near today's Missoula, Montana on July 1, 1806. We do not know whether he gathered a specimen; if so, it did not survive the homeward journey. *Cypripedium montanum* grows in the mountains of Washington, Idaho, Montana, and British Columbia and, rarely, in Alaska, California, Colorado and Oregon.

# Bibliography

Craighead, J. J., F. C. Craighead, Jr. with R. J. Davis
*A Field Guide to Rocky Mountain Wildflowers*
Boston, Houghton Mifflin Co., 1963

Coulter, J. M.
*Manual of the Botany of the Rocky Mountain Region*
New York, American Book Co., 1885

Davis, R. J.
*Flora of Idaho*
Dubuque, IA, Wm. C. Brown Company,1952, reprinted 1955

Duff, J. F. and R. K. Moseley
*Alpine Wildflowers of the Rocky Mountains*
Missoula, Mountain Press Publishing Company, 1989

Earle, A. S. & J. L. Reveal
*Lewis and Clark's Green World: The Expedition and Its Plants*
Helena, MT, Farcountry Press, 2003

Flora of North America Editorial Committee
*Flora of North America North of Mexico* (30 vols.)
vols. 1, 3-5, 19-23
New York, Oxford University Press, 1993

Gledhill, D.
*The Names of Plants* (3d Ed)
Cambridge, UK, Cambridge University Press, 2002

Harrington, H. D.
*Edible Native Plants of the Rocky Mountains*
Albuquerque, NM, University of New Mexico Press, 1967

Hitchcock, C. L. and A. Cronquist
*Flora of the Pacific Northwest, An Illustrated Manual*
Seattle, WA, University of Washington Press, 1973

Hitchcock, C. L., et al.
*Vascular Plants of the Pacific Northwest*
Seattle, WA,University of Washington Press, 5 vols. 1955, 7th
printing 1994 with corrections.

Kershaw, L., A. McKinnon, J. Pojar
*Plants of the Rocky Mountains*
Edmonton, AB, Lone Pine Publishing, 1998

Mabberly, D. J.
*The Plant Book: A Portable Dictionary of Vascular Plants* (2d Ed.)
Cambridge, UK, Cambridge University Press, 1997
reprinted with corrections 1998, 2000

Niehaus, T. F. and C. L. Ripper
*Peterson Field Guide to Pacific State Wildflowers*
Boston, Houghton Mifflin Co., 1987

Philips, H. W.
*Central Rocky Mountain Wildflowers,* and
*Northern Rocky Mountain Wildflowers*
Helena, MT, Falcon Publishing Company, 1999, 2001

Schreier, C.
*A Field Guide to Wildflowers of the Rocky Mountains*
Moose, WY, Homestead Publishing, 1996

Strickler, D.
*Forest Wildflowers,*
*Alpine Wildflowers*
*Wayside Wildflowers of the Pacific Northwest*
Columbia Falls, MT, Flower Press, 1988, 1990, 1993

Strickler, D.
*Northwest Penstemons*
Columbia Falls, MT, Flower Press, , 1997

Reveal, J. L. & J. S. Pringle. *Taxonomic botany and floristics*
Flora of North America Editorial Committee (ed.), in *Flora*
*of North America North of Mexico* Vol. 1, pp. 157-192
New York, Oxford University Press, 1993

Whitson, T. D., et al.
*Weeds of the West,* 5th Ed.
Jackson Hole, WY, University of Wyoming, 1996

Zwinger, A. H. and B. E. Willard
*Land Above the Trees: A Guide to Ameirican Alpine Tundra*
New York, Harper & Row, 1972

*Oxford English Dictionary* (2d Ed. on CDROM version 3.0)
New York, Oxford University Press, 2002

## Useful Web Sites

*California Plant Names*
www.calflora.net/botanicalnames/

*Dictionary of Botanical Epithets*
www.winternet.com/~chuckg/dictionary.html
usda/fnach7.html

USDA Plants Database (http://plants.usda.gov/)

# Index